Killer Slippers

AND HOW TO MAKE THEM

Killer Slippers

AND HOW TO MAKE THEM
by
Nick Godlee

RAINCOAST BOOKS

Vancouver

First published in Canada in 1997 by
Raincoast Books
8680 Cambie Street
Vancouver, B.C. V6P 6M9
(604) 323-7100

Created and produced by The Watermark Press, Sydney
© The Watermark Press 1997
Slipper designs © Nicholas Godlee 1997

Canadian Cataloguing in Publication Data

Godlee, Nick.
   Killer slippers and how to make them

   ISBN 1-55192-106-5.

   1. Footwear. 2. Handicraft. I. Title.

TT678.5.G62 1997   646.4   C97-910484-X

Typeset in 12/16 pt Perpetua
Printed in China

Acknowledgements

After the fulsome tributes paid to *Killer Tea Cosies* (not to mention three reprints), we swiftly signed up Nick Godlee to produce these *Killer Slippers* before he returned to making costumes for the movies. What a brilliant job he has made of them.

Other assistance in the final production of this book came from Simon Blackall (who modelled his legs in the cover shot) and Diane Wallis (who modestly modelled hers within the book). Sophie Blackall drew the diagrams which help explain how to make each slipper. Annette Wallis was once again a methodical editor who checked and deciphered the instructions and Siobhan O'Connor painstakingly put the whole book together.

Photography is all by Simon Blackall. The background picture on the cover is *The Wave* by Katsushika Hokusai and the location for the swan photograph was the Nell Wallis Memorial Garden.

Last, but not least, the introductory text to each pair of slippers was written by Leith Hillard, with interjections by Simon Blackall.

Our Fleet of Foot

First Steps 9

Babar & Celeste 14

The Tubers 22

Dream Feet 28

Footsy & Tootsy 34

Les Petits Déjeuners 40

Frani & Pani 46

The Citroën Twins 50

The Fins 58

Tutti & Frutti 66

Push & Pull 70

Seen on the Rialto 80

Buzz & Swat 86

Way down upon the … 94

The Missionary Decision 100

Initial Pleasures 108

FIRST STEPS

■ Throughout this book, most pattern pieces do not include seam allowance. Written instructions indicate how much to add.

■ The parts of the foot referred to in the written instructions and labels on patterns are indicated directly below in the two foot illustrations.

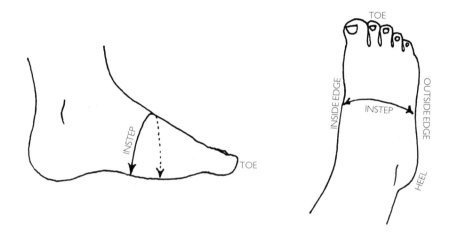

COVERING SLIPPERS

■ Cutting instructions for covers for slippers are for making a pair of each pattern piece. Methods are for making one slipper only at a time.

MATERIALS

Calico (muslin), paper, tracing paper and tracing wheel,
thin wadding, fabric glue

EQUIPMENT

Scissors, pins, hand sewing needles, thread, pen or pencil
to draw on calico and paper, fabric marking pencil, tape measure
or ruler, sewing machine

METHOD 1: BACKLESS SLIPPER

MAKING PATTERN

■ Drape a piece of calico over
slipper and pin in place
firmly, but not tightly.
With fingertips, press
firmly to determine the junction of fabric
upper and sole of slipper. Draw around the
outline of fabric area of slipper to produce a
shape something like this.

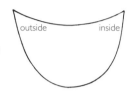

■ Cut out this shape and trace onto paper,
marking the inside and outside edges of
foot. Add 1.5 cm (⅝ in) seam allowance
on all edges. Indicate the outside edge
with a notch on the instep edge.

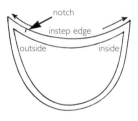

CUTTING OUT

■ To cut a pair, fold fabric for the covering in half, over this place
the carbon paper with the paper pattern on top. Using a tracing
wheel, trace around the edge of the paper pattern then cut out on
this line, marking notch. The folded fabric will give you a right and
left foot pattern piece and the cut out fabric includes seam allowance.

COVERING

■ Press all seam allowances towards the
wrong side of fabric and tack in place,
clipping curves, where necessary.

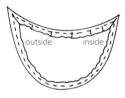

■ Place a thin layer of wadding over the area of
slipper to be covered and trim it about 1.5 cm (⅝ in) in from the
edge. Tack or glue in place. Pin fabric cover in position and glue or
hand stitch it down carefully.

METHOD 2: FULL SLIPPER WITHOUT ELASTIC

MAKING PATTERN

■ Following Method 1 on page 10, drape calico over front and draw outline. Repeat for inside back and outside back panels. They will look something like this.

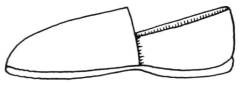

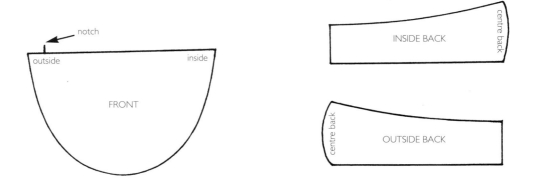

■ Trace pieces onto paper, marking inside and outside edges of foot on Front and centre back on Inside Back and Outside Back. Add 1.5 cm (⅝ in) seam allowance to all edges and notch instep edge of Front to show outside edge.

CUTTING OUT

■ Following Method 1 on page 10, cut one pair of each piece. With marking pencil on wrong side of fabric, label each piece with its name and whether it is for a left or right slipper. Keep left and right pieces separate. To avoid confusion, you may find it preferable to work on only one slipper at a time

COVERING

■ On the top edges of an Inside Back and Outside Back, press the seam allowance to the wrong side and tack. With right sides together, machine stitch Inside Back and Outside Back to Front, pressing seams open. Press top edge of Front to wrong side and tack.

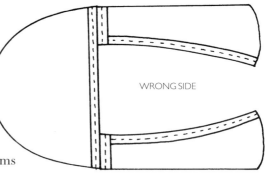

■ Fit cover on slipper, adjusting back seam to fit. Sew back seam. Press up lower edge and tack. Pin cover over slipper and glue or sew in place. Repeat for other slipper

Note: If the top edge is to be finished with binding, omit the seam allowance on the top edge. Another method of finishing the top edge is to turn the seam allowance to below the binding on the slipper and stitch in place leaving the slipper binding showing.

METHOD 3: SLIPPER WITH ELASTIC INSERT

MAKING PATTERN

■ Follow Method 2 on page 11 to make patterns for Front (using the fabric edge and not the elastic as your guide line), Inside Back and Outside Back. They will look like this.

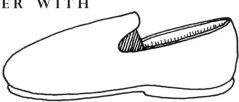

■ Cut out the shapes and trace onto paper, marking inside and outside edges of Front and labelling the Inside Back and Outside Back pieces. Add 1.5 cm (⅝ in) seam allowance on all edges. Indicate the outside edge of Front with a notch on the instep edge (see left). Then trace a Facing pattern for the instep edge of Front (see right).

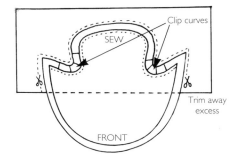

CUTTING OUT

■ Following Method 1 on page 10, cut a pair of each piece.

COVERING

■ With right sides together, join Facing to Front along the instep edge, trim away excess, clip corners and curves and turn right side out. Press seam allowance on top edge of Inside Back and Outside Back to wrong side and tack. Pin Front over Inside Back and Outside Back and topstitch along the instep edge of Front, catching in the Back pieces as you sew.

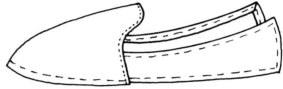

■ Complete as for Method 2 on page 11.

Babar
&
Celeste

There's no business like shoe business! Come thrill to the eath-shattering performance of these pachyderms as they trip the heavy fantastic. This pair are real shoe stoppers who never forget their steps. When they go through the hoops, they do it together or, tusk, tusk, they'll be out of the ring before the fat lady trumpets … and no trunk calls.

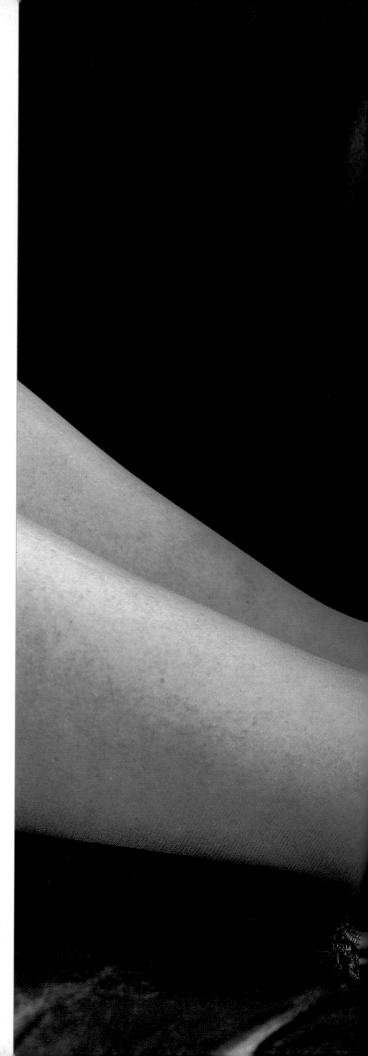

INSTRUCTIONS

MATERIALS

pair of backless slippers

70 cm (¾ yd) grey stonewashed cotton fabric

30 cm (⅓ yd) red velvet

10 cm (4 in) blue felt

30 cm (⅓ yd) heavyweight non-fusible,

non-woven interfacing e.g. Vilene

small piece dark grey felt about 10 cm (4 in) square

small scrap pink felt

small piece white vinyl or leather

four eyes, 7.5 mm (⁵⁄₁₆ in) diameter

grey thread

desired trims for slipper and ring

1.10 m (1¼ yd) synthetic boning or Rigeline

4 short lengths of wire e.g. twist ties from garbage

bags or millinery wire

small bag of polyester fibre filling

The elephant fits a slipper front measuring 21 cm (8¼ in) around the widest part of its opening. For a smaller slipper, use a photocopier to reduce entire elephant pattern to fit.

PREPARING SLIPPERS

■ Following Method 1 on page 10, cover front part of slipper with grey cotton to within 1 cm (⅜ in) of the sole.

■ Prepare a finished 2.5 cm (1 in) wide band of red velvet to an appropriate length by turning under 1 cm (⅜ in) seam allowances on both long sides and glue or sew it just above sole. Depending on the style of slipper, cover just the front or take the band all the way around. Trim with gold braid if desired.

MAKING ELEPHANT BODY

■ On grey cotton fabric, allowing 1 cm (⅜ in) seam allowance, trace pattern pieces. Cut 2 each of Front Gusset and Trunk, 4 of Foot, 2 pairs each of Leg and Side and 4 pairs of Ear. Using a tracing wheel and carbon paper, mark ear, tusk, eye and toenail positions on right side of fabric so that they will be visible when the body is made up. Clip into seam allowance to mark notches.

■ Fold Trunk in half lengthwise with right sides together and stitch from D to G. Join Sides to Front Gusset, stopping exactly at point A. Matching points C, B, A and D, join the Sides to the back portion of the Trunk. Clip all curves then turn right side out.

■ Join Ears in pairs with right sides together, leaving a gap between H and I. Clip into corners and turn to right side.

■ Make up leg by folding lengthwise with right sides together and stitching from X to Y. Clip about 7 mm (¼ mm) into seam allowance on straight edge from Y to Y then pin to right side of Foot. Join seam on stitching line. Turn to right side and fill firmly.

FEATURES

■ At mark on each Side, cut a small hole and insert an eye, sliding keeper on to back of eye

■ From pink felt cut out Trunk End and Inner Mouth.

■ From grey felt, cut out Lower Mouth, Eyelids, Tusk Bases.

■ Make up mouth by sewing or gluing pink felt to grey felt taking care that there is a tiny bit of grey showing around the pink. Glue or hand stitch the mouth to Gusset at mark.

■ Fill Trunk lightly and Body a little more firmly.

■ To make Tusk, cut 4 of Tusk from white leather.

■ Place a piece of wire along the length of wrong side of Tusk, using wire double if it is very fine, fold Tusk lengthwise and sew or glue raw edges together.

■ Glue or sew Tusk to Side at mark.

■ Glue grey felt Tusk Base over the base of the tusk.

■ Glue or sew Eyelids to eye.

■ Turn in end of Trunk and glue or sew Trunk End into tip of Trunk.

■ From red velvet, cut out Star and glue or sew to forehead.

■ From white leather, cut Toenails and glue or sew to Leg over foot seam. Fold Leg at bend mark and catch it in bent position with hand stitching.

■ Arrange Ears on Side where marked and sew between H and I, catching the gap closed as you sew.

FINISHING OFF ELEPHANT

■ Turn under 1 cm (⅜ in) on lower edge and sew elephant to slipper.

■ Position a Leg on each side of elephant so that one is a little higher than the other.

■ Turn under open edges and sew the Legs in place.

■ Run a gathering thread along middle section of trunk and draw up so that Trunk bends upwards. Secure thread firmly.

HOOP

■ Cut a length of the boning to make a circle which sits comfortably around elephant. Glue or bind the ends together to make a hoop.

From the interfacing cut a circle about 2.5 cm (1 in) larger than the hoop. Fold interfacing edges over the outside of the hoop and glue or sew in place, trimming off excess. Glue a strip of blue felt around edge of the hoop and add any other trims to decorate. Cut about seven equally spaced slashes from centre to edge of hoop. Place over elephant and glue or sew in place.

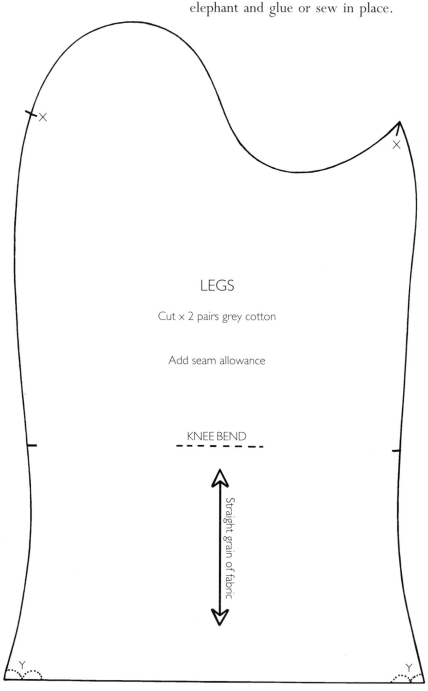

LEGS

Cut x 2 pairs grey cotton

Add seam allowance

KNEE BEND

Straight grain of fabric

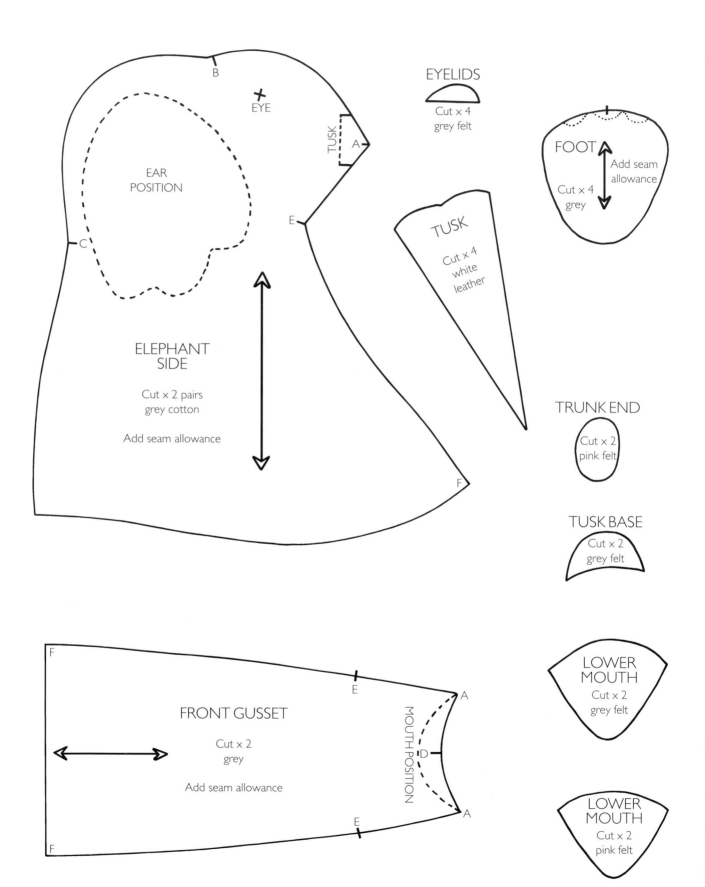

EYELIDS
Cut × 4
grey felt

FOOT
Add seam allowance
Cut × 4 grey

TUSK
Cut × 4 white leather

B

EYE

TUSK

A

EAR POSITION

C

E

ELEPHANT SIDE

Cut × 2 pairs grey cotton

Add seam allowance

F

TRUNK END
Cut × 2 pink felt

TUSK BASE
Cut × 2 grey felt

F

FRONT GUSSET

Cut × 2 grey

Add seam allowance

E

MOUTH POSITION

A

D

A

E

F

LOWER MOUTH
Cut × 2 grey felt

LOWER MOUTH
Cut × 2 pink felt

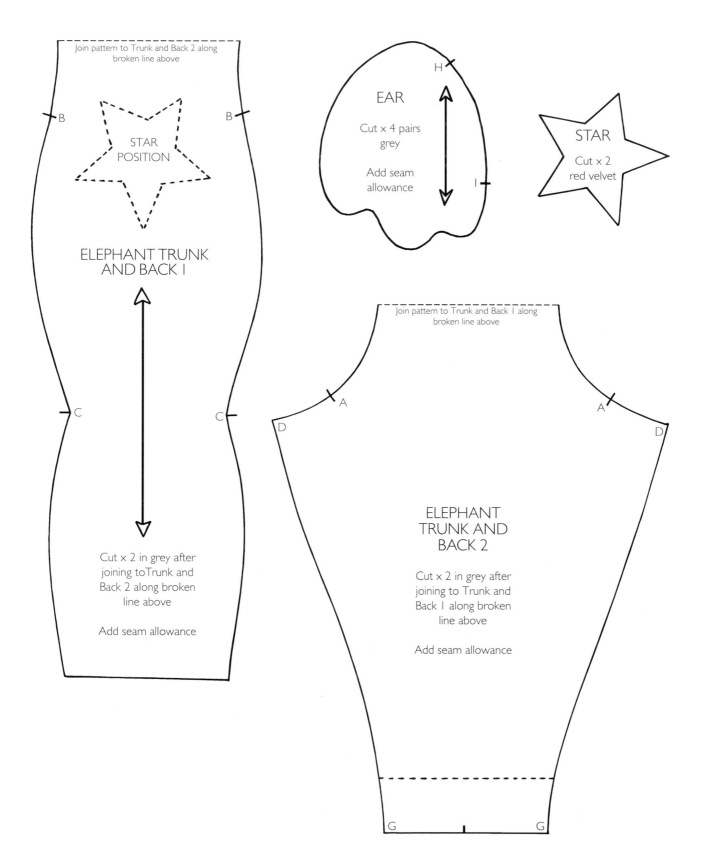

Join pattern to Trunk and Back 2 along broken line above

B   B

STAR
POSITION

ELEPHANT TRUNK
AND BACK 1

C   C

Cut x 2 in grey after
joining to Trunk and
Back 2 along broken
line above

Add seam allowance

EAR

Cut x 4 pairs
grey

Add seam
allowance

H

I

STAR

Cut x 2
red velvet

Join pattern to Trunk and Back 1 along
broken line above

A   A

D   D

ELEPHANT
TRUNK AND
BACK 2

Cut x 2 in grey after
joining to Trunk and
Back 1 along broken
line above

Add seam allowance

G   G

The Tubers

And so the proverbial couch potatoes hit the sack. Tubers take root in front of the tube and search for soupy soap operas. "The Sack of Troy" or perhaps a film from Swedeland? But of course they settle for "MASH".

When the chips are down, they're going to fry! Now that's a turnip for the books.

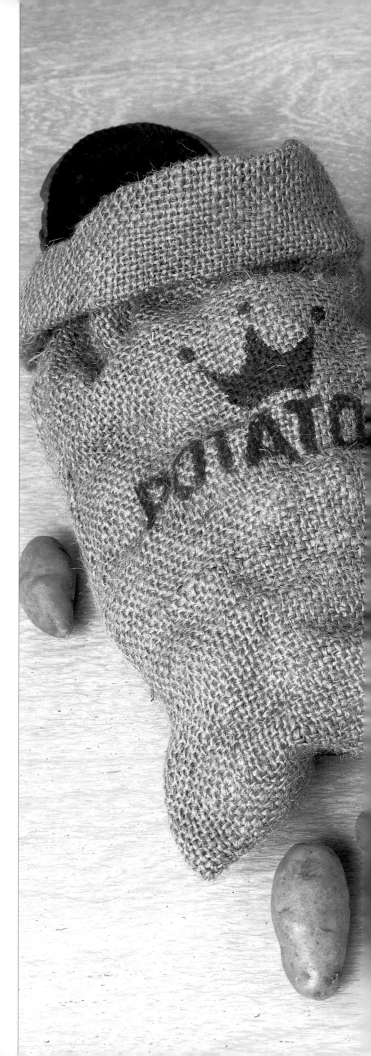

INSTRUCTIONS

MATERIALS

pair of backless slippers

40 cm (½ yd) hessian sacking and thread to match

17 polystyrene foam balls 3 cm (1¼ in) diameter

red and blue fabric printing ink

letter stencils 2 cm (¾ in) high from newsagents or stationers

10 cm (4 in) square of thin cardboard

hot glue gun and glue

■ Measure across widest part of slipper. Call this measurement 'A'.

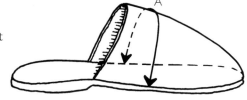

■ Measure from toe of slipper to point farthest back on upper of slipper. Call this measurement 'B'.

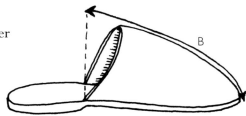

■ On paper, make a pattern for the sack thus.

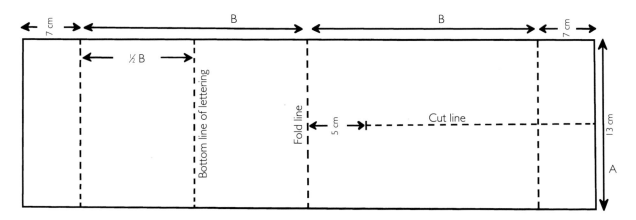

■ From hessian, cut out a sack and make markings from pattern with marking chalk or pencil.

■ Using the letter stencil and a sponge dipped lightly into the red ink, print the word 'Potatoes' centred on the guide line. Fill in the gaps left by the stencil with a sharp corner of sponge dipped in ink.

■ Trace the crown pattern onto cardboard and cut out the crown leaving a silhouette. Use this stencil to print in blue ink just above the centre of Potatoes. Allow ink to dry and set as directed on ink container.

■ Fold hessian along foldline with right sides together. Stitch along both sides from foldline to 10 cm (4 in) from top of bag. Clip seam allowance to point where sewing ends.

■ Turn bag to right side so that printing is showing. Stitch the remaining 10 cm (4 in) on either side of bag with wrong sides together. Press seams open.

■ Cut along cut line as marked on pattern.

■ Cut foam balls in half with knife or scissors. Using half the hemispheres for each sack, carefully apply glue to the highest point of the curved side and stick to the wrong side of the printed top of the sack. Arrange in a random fashion between the Crown and the foldline.

■ Fold top 2.5 cm (1 in) of sack to right side then fold again 3.5 cm (1⅜ in) from first fold.

■ Place sack on top of slipper. Tuck in all hessian so that none will hang below the sole. Glue tucked in hessian to slipper just above sole but leave opening free.

■ Dampen hessian with a hand sprayer and mould over the balls so they look more distinct. Allow to dry.

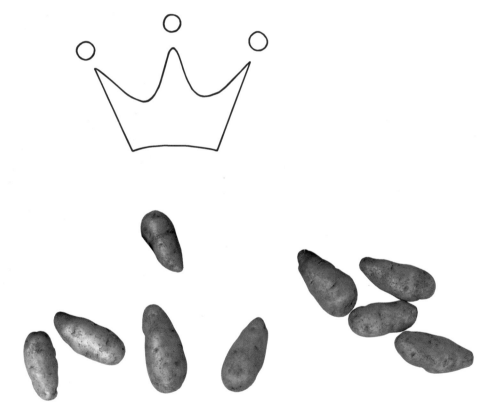

Dream
Feet

These luxurious loafers indulge the sleepwalker in all of us, cradling the weary foot and covering it with an eiderdown to counterpain.

For those who want to turn in without risking knock knees and pigeon toes; who long to spring up without fearing a sprained ankle, this pair comfortably sleeps two.

INSTRUCTIONS

MATERIALS

pair of backless slippers

30 cm (12 in) cotton or wool blanket like fabric

20 cm (8 in) medium weight white cotton fabric

scrap ticking fabric

small amounts of pale blue, pale green and white felt

white thread

dark blue thread

dark green thread

scrap of thin wadding

PATTERNS

■ Following Method 1 on page 10, make pattern for covering slipper.

■ For Bottom Sheet trace cover pattern from instep and cut across 5 cm from centre instep edge. For Top Sheet and Blanket, trace from toe up and cut off 2.5 cm (1 in) from instep edge in a straight line. Pieces will overlap by 2.5 cm (1 in).

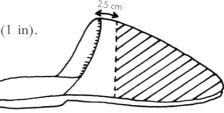

BOTTOM SHEET

■ Add 1 cm (⅜ in) seam allowance to the Bottom Sheet pattern and cut 2 pairs from white fabric. Place a pair right sides together and stitch around, leaving straight edge open. Clip corners and curves, turn to the right side. Glue or sew the Bottom Sheet in place on slipper making sure to cover the instep edge.

BLANKET AND TOP SHEET

■ From blanket fabric cut a pair from pattern, adding 2 cm (¾ in) seam allowance to curved edges where fabric of slipper meets the

sole. From white fabric, cut two 7 cm
(2¾ in) wide binding strips the length
of the straight top edge of the
blanket. Fold binding strip 2 cm
(¾ in) from one long edge and press
then fold again 2 cm (¾ in) from first
fold and press. Place binding over
top edge of blanket with 2 cm (¾ in)
wide folded edge on right side and
raw edge on wrong side. Topstitch
close to fold edge, using white thread.
Position the Blanket over the slipper with
the Top Sheet edge 2.5 cm (1 in) from the instep edge of the Bottom
Sheet and pin in place. Turn under raw edges and glue or sew to
slipper leaving top sheet edge loose like a real bed.

PILLOW

■ From white cotton, cut out Pillow Case. Fold, right sides together
on centre Fold shown on pattern and with 1 cm (⅜ in) seam
allowance, stitch across one end and along side. Turn to right side.
On raw edge turn under Foldlines and topstitch close to edge.

■ Cut out Wadding piece.

■ From ticking, cut out Pillow piece. With right sides together, fold
Pillow on foldline stitch along each side with 1 cm (⅜ in) seam
allowance. Turn to right side and insert the end of the Wadding piece
into the Pillow. Glue lightly or sew to secure. Push open end of
Pillow into Pillow Case with Pillow protruding about 0.5 cm (³⁄₁₆ in)
and secure with glue inside pillow case edge.

HOT WATER BOTTLE

■ Trace pattern onto felt. Place felt (pattern side up) over a piece of
wadding. Using dark blue thread, machine quilt circle in centre,
radiating lines, curve above circle and straight line of top.

■ Place another piece of blue felt underneath and sew remaining lines except for the curved edge at the very top. Trim about 2 mm (¹⁄₁₆ in) from the outside edge all the way around Hot Water Bottle and trim straight edge of front of opening. Mark the little dots at the top and bottom and push a little filling or wadding through the neck of bottle with a skewer or fine knitting needle. Do not overfill as bottle should be fairly flat.

BOOK

■ Mark Book Cover pattern onto single layer of green felt. Cut out Book Spine and topstitch it to Book Cover. Place another piece of green felt underneath and stitch around the Book Cover shape. Satinstitch or hand embroider the 'A' onto the book.

■ From white felt, cut out Book Pages pattern and concertina along fold lines as shown. Glue edge with three folds inside spine area of Book Cover. Other edge with ends and two folds will protrude from the Book Cover so trim these just a little smaller than the Book Cover to form pages.

TO FINISH OFF

■ Glue or sew the pillows, book and water bottle onto beds.

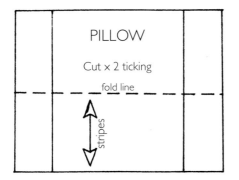

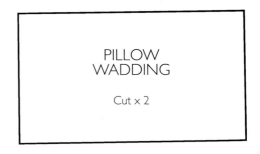

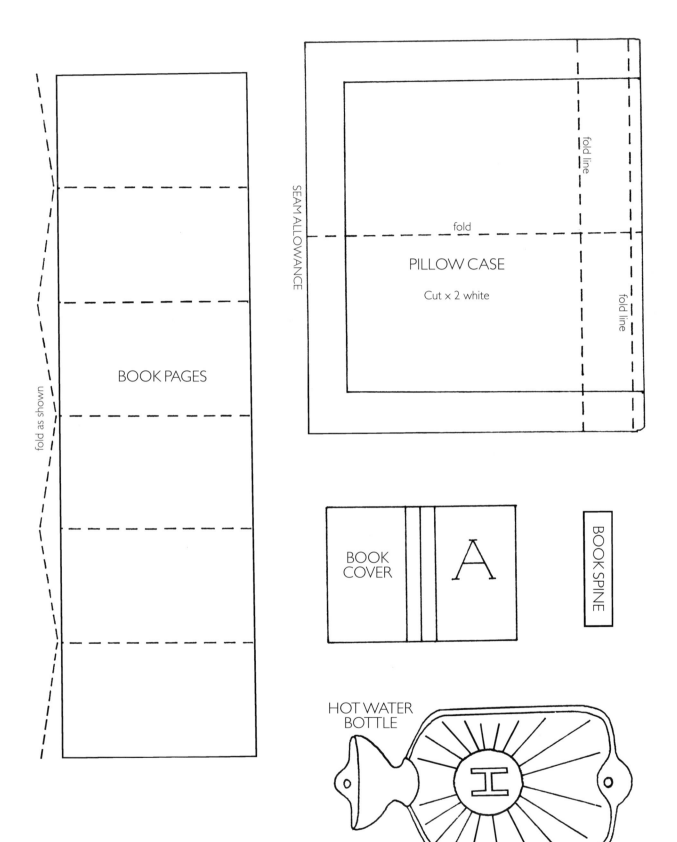

fold as shown

BOOK PAGES

SEAM ALLOWANCE

fold line

fold

fold line

PILLOW CASE

Cut x 2 white

BOOK
COVER

A

BOOK SPINE

HOT WATER
BOTTLE

Footsy
&
Tootsy

An ideal design for a fast and loose game of footsy, these slippers will also keep you instep. If you've outgrown ingrown toe-nails and wish to resurrect some arches that have fallen by the wayside, turn your Achilles heel into an athlete's foot with this wearfoot footwear.

Now turn your foot loose for a quickstep. This pair moves at a blistering-free pace.

INSTRUCTIONS

MATERIALS

pair of full slippers

50 cm (20 in) skin colour felt

1 piece firm, flexible translucent plastic (from some fabric stores,

usually used for quilting templates)

small amount of polyester fibre filling

masking tape

pink and black fabric printing inks or paints

skin coloured thread

scrap of skin coloured knit fabric (if slippers have elastic insert)

skin coloured bias tape 25 mm (1 in) wide finished

30 cm (12 in) thin wadding

20 cm (8 in) calico or any scrap fabric

COVERING SLIPPERS

■ Following Method 2 on page 11 or Method 3 on page 12, make a cover pattern for the slippers. Using photocopier, adjust the Foot Front pattern until it fits into the toe area of the Front Slipper Cover pattern and trace the toes and details onto the pattern. From felt, cut out a pair of each of the Front, Inside Back and Outside Back Cover pattern with 2.5 cm (1 in) seam allowances. Mark toes and details on to the right side of Front. Flop the foot details pattern for the right slipper.

TOENAILS

■ On Front, paint toenail areas pink. Using sharp scissors, cut along the curved edge of the toenail area. Do not cut the straight edge.

■ For each toenail cut out a rectangle of plastic about 5 mm ($\frac{3}{16}$ in) bigger than the toenail area shown with dotted line on pattern. Stick a strip of masking tape just under the front edge of the piece to suggest the white edge of the toenail and trim off excess tape.

■ On the opposite side of the big toenail stick a semi-circle of masking tape to the underside to look like a half moon when the toenail is inserted.

■ From the wrong side of the Front slip the toenail over the flap of the toenail area. Topstitch the nail in place around the curve of the skin colour felt but not across the front edge. From the wrong side, trim edge of toenail to about 4 mm (⅛ in) from stitching.

TOES

■ Place front shaped piece of calico under the Front, with instep edge at least 2 cm (¾ in) towards instep from toe bases and topstitch around the toes.

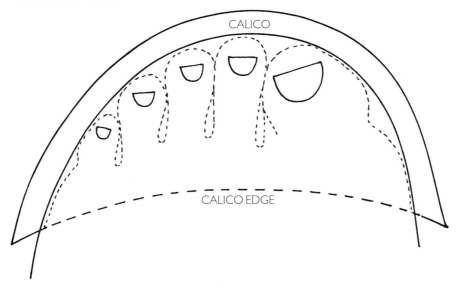

■ From the wrong side, fill the toes fairly firmly with polyester fibre. Form the toe joint creases with long hand stitches.

■ Paint the spaces between the toes pink.

TO FINISH OFF

■ Place a layer of thin wadding over the whole of the slipper, trimming just inside the edges. Fit the felt to the slipper and mark the seam allowances. Glue binding around top edge of slipper. Join pieces of cover, Sides to Front and centre Back seam and press the seams allowances on the edges under. To cover elastic inserts, slip a folded piece of the knit fabric under the part of the cover over the elastic area of the slipper and top stitch in place.

■ Put the cover over the slipper and glue down edges.

■ Paint the area between the toes and the sole with black.

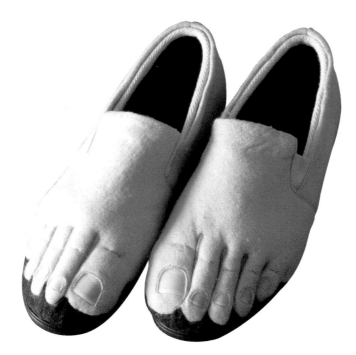

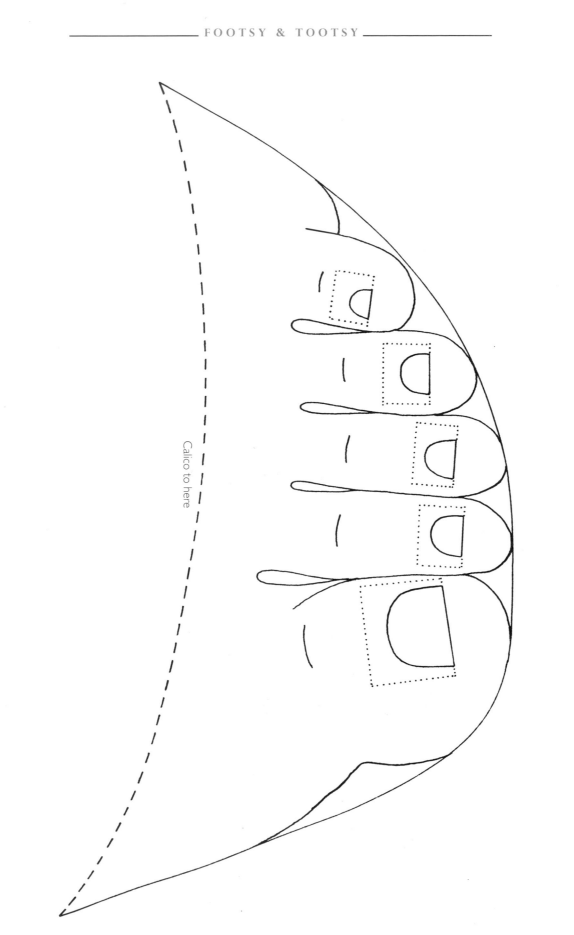

Calico to here

Les Petits Déjeuners

The weekend comes. It's time to get out of the Monday to Friday grinder, break out of the fast lane and relax. But first, bring in the newspaper, put your feet up and savour the delicatessence of life. Conjure up a croissant, balance a baguette, and sit back and smell the coffee. For you, it's café *olé* all the way.

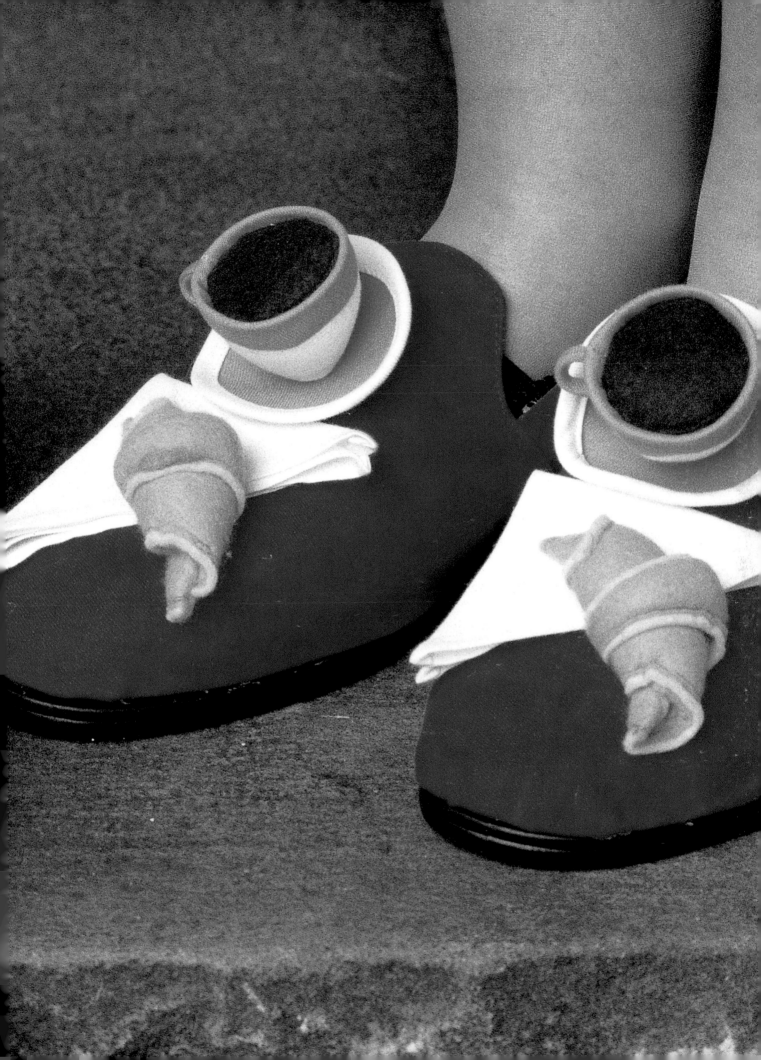

INSTRUCTIONS

MATERIALS

pair of full slippers with elastic inserts

60 cm (⅔ yd) red fabric to cover slippers

10 cm (4 in) blue cotton fabric

20 cm (8 in) (¼ yd) white cotton fabric

scrap dark brown felt

10 cm (4 in) dark gold felt

10 cm (4 in) light gold felt

scrap of buckram or other very stiff material

small amount of polyester fibre filling — enough to

fill cups and croissant

20 (¼ yd) cm medium weight iron-on interfacing

PREPARING SLIPPERS

■ Following Method 3 on page 12, cut out slipper covers and facings from red fabric as well as 2 bias strips 3 cm (1¼ in) wide and 28 cm long. Press under 1 cm (⅜ in) seam allowances on short ends of bias strips. Do not press the seam allowance at the top of the Inside Back and Outside Back to the wrong side. Instead, once the back seam has been fitted and joined, with right sides together and a 1 cm (⅜ in) seam allowance, machine stitch a bias strip to the top edge of the back section of the cover assembly, aligning the strip's centre with the centre back seam of cover. When covering the slipper, turn the bias strip over the slipper edge and, with a 1 cm (⅜ in) turn under, either glue or hand stitch its edge to the lining of the slipper. Repeat for other slipper.

CUP AND SAUCER

■ Following instructions on patterns, cut out pieces for two cups and saucers, adding 5 mm (¼ in) seam allowance unless otherwise indicated.

■ Iron interfacing to wrong side of Cup and Lip.

■ Fold Lip in half lengthwise and press.

■ Join one long edge of Lip to long edge of Cup using interfacing edges as seam lines. Press seam towards Cup.

■ Fold Handle in half lengthwise and press, open out, fold edges to foldline and press then fold in half again.

■ Handsew edges together.

■ Pin one end of Handle to Lip 3 mm (⅛ in) above seamline.

■ With right sides together join side seam of Cup and Lip, catching in Handle. Press seam open.

■ Turn Lip to inside and topstitch from the right side just below seamline using white thread.

■ Turn under free end of Handle and catch to Cup 17 mm (¾ in) down from top of white.

■ Turn bottom seam allowance to wrong side and topstitch just beside fold line.

■ Sew buckram to centre of Coffee. Turn under and press seam allowance.

■ Hand stitch Coffee into Cup about 5 mm (¼ in) from edge of Lip.

■ Iron interfacing to Saucer.

■ Press saucer Rim in half down length. Open out and press edges towards centre fold. Open out then join ends right sides together and press seam open. Fold Rim again and stretch around edge of Saucer and topstitch through all layers.

CROISSANT

■ Following instructions on pattern, cut pieces for two Croissants.

■ Place a dark piece on a light piece, so that about 3 mm (⅛ in) of light shows around pointed end of dark.

■ Topstitch about 2 mm (just under ⅛ in) from edge of dark piece leaving flat end open.

■ Using pattern as a guide, place a pin at first broken line from pointed end of pattern. Push a little filling to where pin is and place a pin at next broken line. Repeat for the next filled area.

■ Fold dark edge over end of light and topstitch in place.

■ Roll up croissant, folding at positions of pins to form a flat bottom and rounded top. Hand stitch to secure and remove pins.

NAPKIN

■ From white fabric, cut two 13 cm (5 in) squares. Narrow hem edges. Fold diagonally into triangle and fold again.

FINISHING OFF

■ Fill Cup loosely then glue or sew to saucer.

■ Using the photograph as a guide, position cup and saucer, croissant and napkin on covered slipper and sew or glue in place.

Straight grain of fabric

SAUCER RIM

Cut x 2 white cotton
with seam allowance

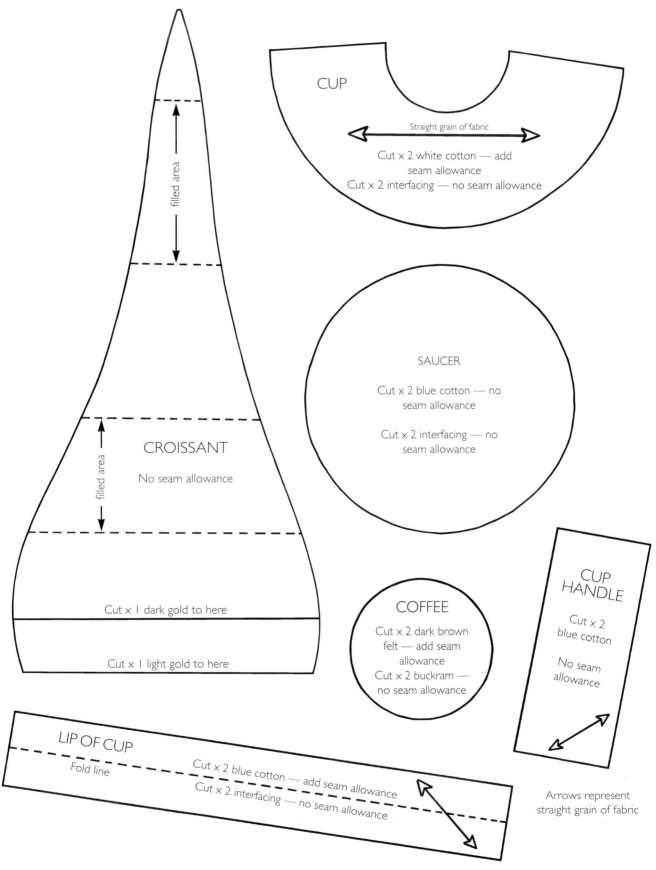

CUP

Straight grain of fabric

Cut × 2 white cotton — add
seam allowance
Cut × 2 interfacing — no seam allowance

SAUCER

Cut × 2 blue cotton — no
seam allowance

Cut × 2 interfacing — no
seam allowance

filled area

CROISSANT

No seam allowance

filled area

Cut × 1 dark gold to here

Cut × 1 light gold to here

COFFEE

Cut × 2 dark brown
felt — add seam
allowance
Cut × 2 buckram —
no seam allowance

**CUP
HANDLE**

Cut × 2
blue cotton

No seam
allowance

LIP OF CUP

Fold line

Cut × 2 blue cotton — add seam allowance
Cut × 2 interfacing — no seam allowance

Arrows represent
straight grain of fabric

Frangi & Pani

This exotic branch of the footwear family is a perennial favourite with the slenderer gender. You may wish to go out on a limb with this pair, but weigh the options carefully: each delicate flower needs tender loving care to guide it through inclement weather. We trust you've twigged to the moral of our story: if you're winsome, you lose some.

INSTRUCTIONS

MATERIALS

pair of white towelling half slippers or cover a pair white

30 cm (12 in) white felt

white thread

yellow fabric paint

cotton buds

PVC wood glue

refillable plastic trigger pack

■ Cover slippers if necessary.

FLOWERS

■ Make 13 for each medium size slipper.

■ Trace petal pattern in rows onto felt (five for each flower). Cut along rows but not around petals. With cotton bud, dab a little yellow paint at the straight edge of the petal and blend it upwards to about half way up the petal in the shape shown on the pattern with broken lines at right.

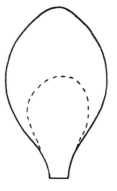

■ Machine stitch a gathering thread around each petal about 3 mm (⅛ in) inside the outline leaving threads long at each end. Cut out the petal just inside the outline. Pull the gathering thread to ease up the sides of the petal just a little. This will give the petal a slight spoon shape. Press the eased areas a little to smooth them and trim off gathering thread ends.

■ Arrange the petals one over another as shown and hand stitch together at the bottom (leaving the thread end attached) then fold the uppermost petal under the lowest petal to complete the sequence. Wind the thread around the centre of the flower a few times to close up the hole.

■ Arrange flowers on slipper and glue or sew in place. Mix glue with an equal quantity of water in the trigger pack and spray the flowers making them quite wet. Allow to dry undisturbed until they are hard.

The Citroën Twins

Slip across the Channel and park yourself in the ergonomic *chaises* of some French classics. Not so much roadsters as loungesters, these souped-up Citröens offer two-on-the-floor transmission from couch to pantry and a bit of *Ooh La! La!* for the young at heart. Special features include naturally aspirated V5s with air suspension, plush interiors and ample room in the rear. Let's go, Jean-Paul.

INSTRUCTIONS

MATERIALS

pair of backless slippers

30 cm (12 in) of 3 mm (⅛ in) wide silver leather trim

40 cm (½ yd) medium weight maroon fabric (body of car)

40 cm (½ yd) black felt

10 cm (4 in) beige felt (dashboard)

30 cm (12 in) wadding

5 cm (2 in) clear plastic (PVC) sheeting (windscreen)

12 cm (5 in) black cord (steering wheel)

4 silver 20 mm (¾ in) buttons for hubcaps

4 buttons 10–17 mm (⅜–¾ in) for headlights

(Take the centre out of a plastic silver military button

and glue in a plastic pearl button.)

10 cm (4 in) silver fabric (silver rubberised lycra)

maroon and beige thread

40 cm (½ yd) fusible wadding about 4 mm (⅛ in) thick

■ Carefully measure distance from centre of instep edge to toe of your slipper to give measurement X–Y. Photocopy pattern with scale line and reduce or enlarge until the scale line is exactly the same length as your measurement X–Y.

■ Using adjusted pattern, take Body pattern piece and place over slipper, matching point X of pattern to point X on the slipper and trace the opening of the slipper if it is different. Add the seam allowance to complete your pattern.

■ From maroon fabric, cut a pair each of Body and Facing. Trim the seam allowance from the Body pattern. From wadding, cut a pair of Body without seam allowance and a pair of each Fender. Position Body wadding on wrong side of Body with Fenders where shown on pattern and hand stitch in place.

■ With right sides together, pin Facing to Body and stitch around edge from A to B. Clip corners and curves and turn to right side.

■ Using beige thread topstitch the lines either side of the hood/bonnet.

■ From PVC, cut out the windscreen. Topstitch silver leather trim to long edge.

■ Cut out dashboard. Fold under the sides and outwardly curved edge. Position on Body catching in Windscreen at foldline and topstitch in place. Fold Windscreen back. Cut two 6 cm (2⅜ in) lengths of black cord and glue to dashboard where marked on pattern.

■ Following Method 1 on page 10, cover front three-quarters of slipper with black felt.

■ Cut out Headlight Bolsters and roll up from one short end in to a cylinder until they are about 7 mm (¼ in) smaller in diameter than the headlight. Cut off excess felt and glue or sew a headlight to one end of each roll.

ATTACHING BODY TO SLIPPER

Turn under the raw edge of Body piece and press. Glue the bonnet/hood area, between lines of topstitching, to the centre of the slipper. Glue the lower edges of fender to the bottom edge of the slipper upper.

■ Slip headlight bolsters into position and glue.

■ Glue body to top edge of slipper.

■ From black felt and silver fabric, cut out Bumper. Place one black and one silver Bumper right sides together and place wadding on silver side and sew along stitching line, leaving open between C and

D. Trim outer edge and clip corners and curves. Turn to right side and press with iron on black side. Glue black felt centre piece into position. Glue bumper to slipper overlapping ends on to fender.

■ Sew silver buttons into wheel gaps.

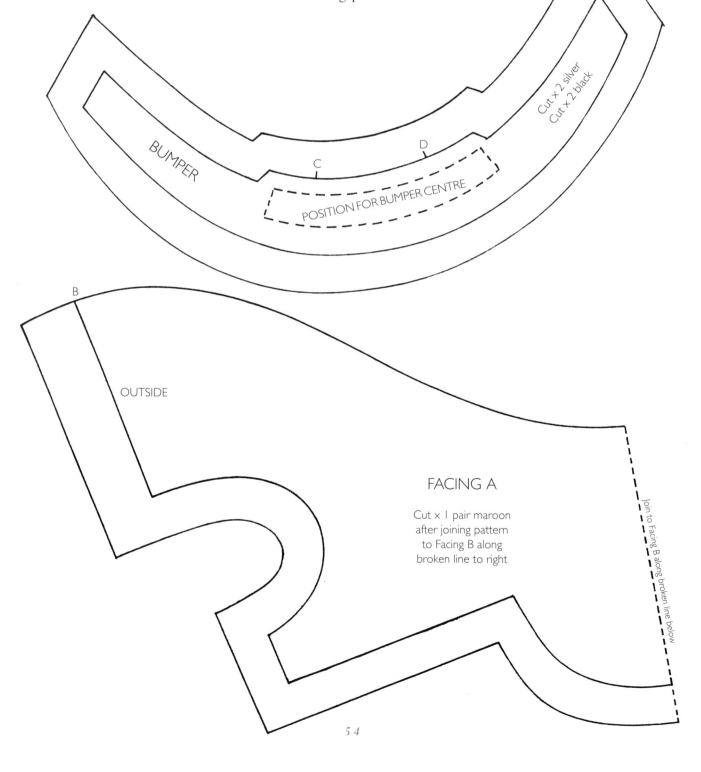

BUMPER

Cut x 2 silver
Cut x 2 black

C

D

POSITION FOR BUMPER CENTRE

B

OUTSIDE

FACING A

Cut x 1 pair maroon
after joining pattern
to Facing B along
broken line to right

Join to Facing B along broken line below

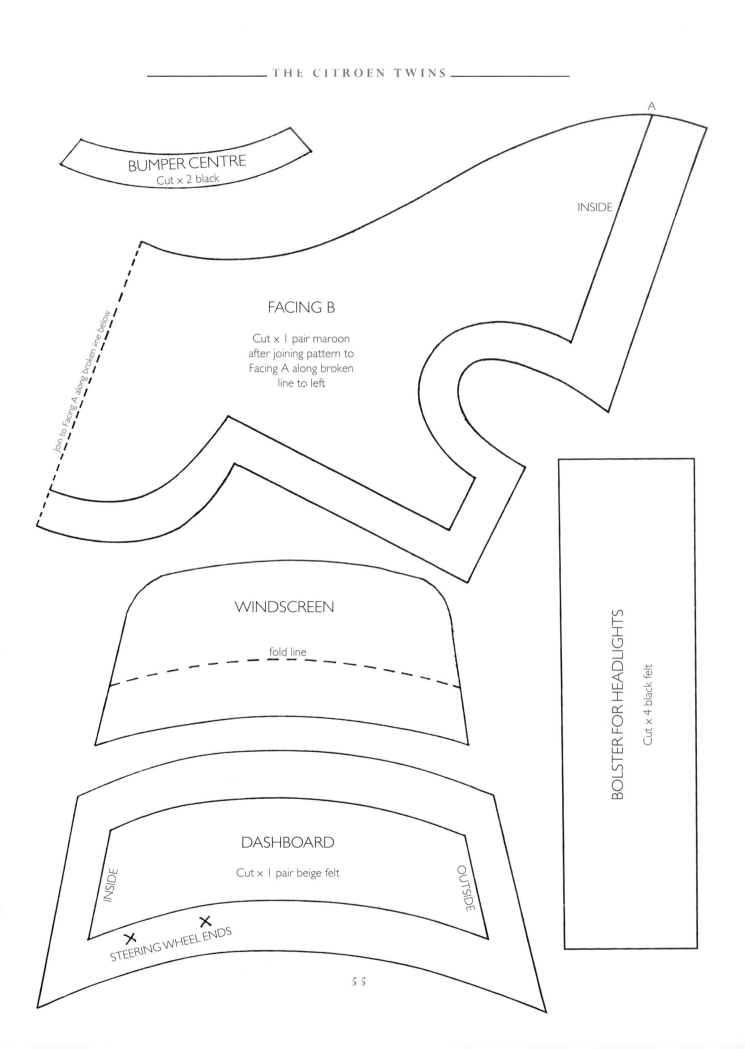

BUMPER CENTRE
Cut x 2 black

A

INSIDE

Join to Facing A along broken line below

FACING B

Cut x I pair maroon
after joining pattern to
Facing A along broken
line to left

WINDSCREEN

fold line

BOLSTER FOR HEADLIGHTS

Cut x 4 black felt

DASHBOARD

Cut x I pair beige felt

INSIDE

OUTSIDE

X

X

STEERING WHEEL ENDS

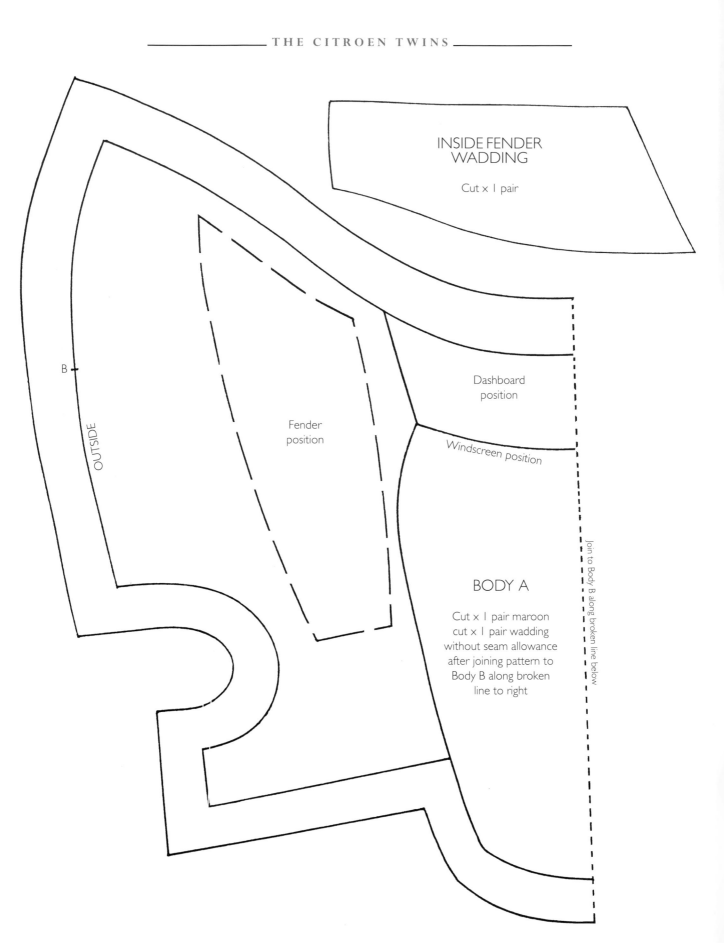

INSIDE FENDER
WADDING

Cut × 1 pair

B

OUTSIDE

Fender
position

Dashboard
position

Windscreen position

BODY A

Cut × 1 pair maroon
cut × 1 pair wadding
without seam allowance
after joining pattern to
Body B along broken
line to right

Join to Body B along broken line below

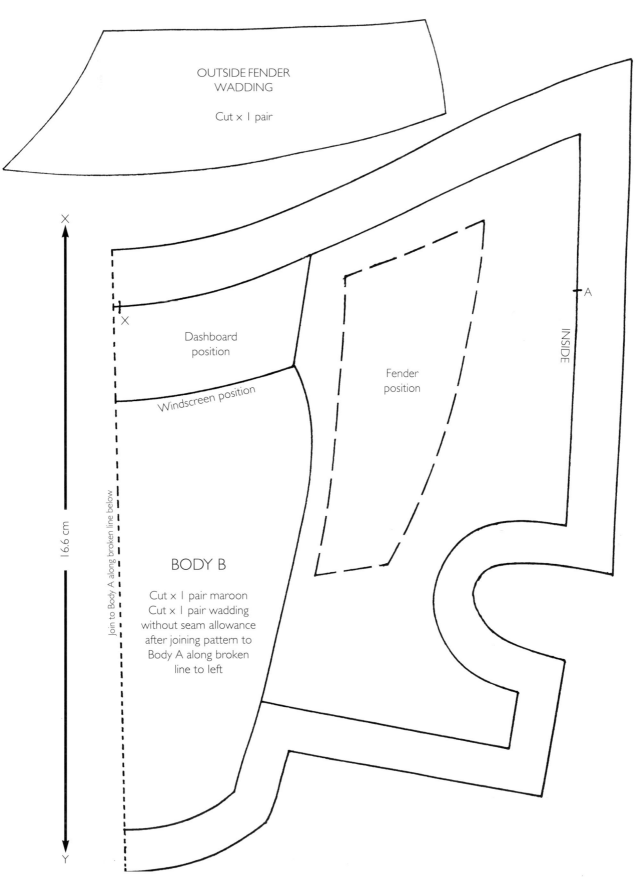

OUTSIDE FENDER
WADDING

Cut x 1 pair

X

X

A

INSIDE

Dashboard
position

Windscreen position

Fender
position

16.6 cm

Join to Body A along broken line below

BODY B

Cut x 1 pair maroon
Cut x 1 pair wadding
without seam allowance
after joining pattern to
Body A along broken
line to left

Y

The Fins

Like the words of the song, it was 'on the road to Mandalay where the flying fishes play' that inspired this frolicsome pair. For those who love to swim against the current style, we recommend the streamlined sole (unbattered) for your heel and toe; a vertebrate for those with a lot of backbone when it comes to fashion. As you reel in the compliments you'll realise you're quite a catch in anyone's brook.

INSTRUCTIONS

MATERIALS

pair of full slippers with or without elastic inserts

60 cm (⅔ yd) green satin (not too stiff)

60 cm (⅔ yd) wadding

4 eyes to fit eye shape on pattern approximately

dark green felt (for fins)

light green fine, shiny fabric (close woven so it

won't fray too much) also for fins

pink satin (for mouth)

clear nail polish or fray stopping product

60 cm (⅔ yd) medium weight non-fusible interfacing

dark green thread

■ With chalk or a marker pen divide the slipper as shown in illustration.

Line A — down the centre of front from instep to toe

Line B — across toe one-sixth length of slipper from point of toe

■ Measure length of line B and add 1 cm (⅜ in) then compare with length of size adjustment line on Head pattern. Use a photocopier to reduce or enlarge the head and all the other fish patterns so the size adjustment is correct length.

■ Following Method 1 on page 10, make a pattern to fit the slipper from line B to the back with a seam along line A. Trace the patterns onto the interfacing twice, flipping them over to trace the second time so that you end up with a mirror-image pair. Cut out allowing 2.5 cm (1 in) around all edges as shrinkage will occur during quilting.

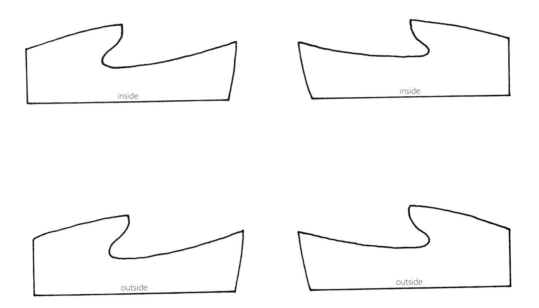

inside   inside

outside   outside

Make a cardboard template by gluing the Scales Template Pattern to some stiff cardboard and cutting around it. Use it to trace scale pattern onto interfacing making sure the scales are facing in the correct direction with round edge to heel of slipper. Place interfacing over wadding with satin underneath, shiny side down. Using a short straight stitch in dark green thread quilt the scales. Repeat for three remaining interfacing sides.

FINS

■ Put a layer of the light green fabric between two layers of dark green felt. Trace Fin patterns onto it with a tracing wheel and carbon paper; for each fish you will need 2 side fins and one each of dorsal and tail fins. Sew along lines shown on fin patterns. Cut out Fin shape outside line. Using small sharp scissors, trim away felt between stitching lines without cutting light green fabric which is the membrane. Paint the raw edge of the light green fabric with nail polish to prevent fraying.

■ Fit Body to slipper (because the assembly will be inside out, fit it on the wrong slipper) by pinning the pieces roughly in place (right sides together) and pinning them to each other along seam lines. Trim seams and lower edge of back to 1 cm (⅜ in). Trim top edge to no seam allowance.

■ Unpin seams and re-pin with right sides together and raw edges matching catching the Dorsal Fin and Tail Fin into the seams. The Tail Fin should sit 2.5 cm (1 in) from the top edge and the Dorsal Fin should sit about 1 cm (⅜ in) from the instep end of the seam. Turn to the right side.

■ Bind top edge all the way around with 4 cm (1⅝ in) wide strip of the green satin cut on the bias unless slippers have elastic inserts. For slippers with elastic inserts, bind edges except the section where the inserts are, then zig zag stitch this section as it will be covered by the Side Fin. Glue the completed body piece onto slipper turning up the lower edge and gluing in place. Glue Side Fins over elastic section if applicable or if there is no elastic glue in a suitable place.

LOWER MOUTH

■ From pink satin and wadding, cut out pair of Lower Mouth noting there is no seam allowance. Place wadding on wrong side of satin and sew together 5 mm (³⁄₁₆ in) from edge.

■ Bind short curve of shape with a 2.8 cm (1⅛ in) wide strip of the green satin bias folded to make a 7 mm (¼ in) wide binding. Glue Lower Mouth to slipper with binding at the toe edge.

HEAD

■ From green satin, cut out four of Head, adding 1 cm (⅜ in) seam allowance. From wadding, cut out two of Head with no seam allowance.

■ Place the wadding pieces on wrong side of one pair of satin Heads and stitch about 5 mm (³⁄₁₆ in) from edge of wadding. With right sides together, place the other Head piece underneath each. Stitch around edges just outside the wadding leaving a gap where shown on pattern.
■ Clip into corner and trim seams to 5 mm (³⁄₁₆ in). Turn to the right side and catch gap closed.

■ Cut holes for eyes where marked and attach eyes. Topstitch upper lip line. Place Head piece on slipper so that there are no gaps on the back of the head, the bottom edges overlap the sole of the slipper and the mouth gapes open. Glue in place.

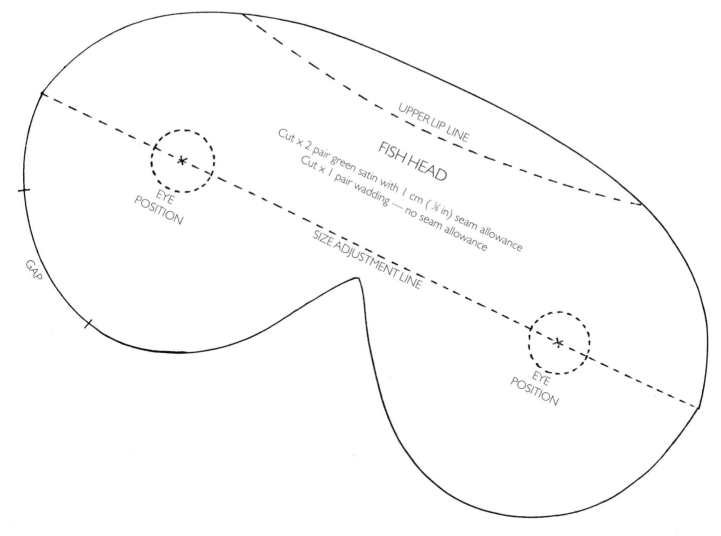

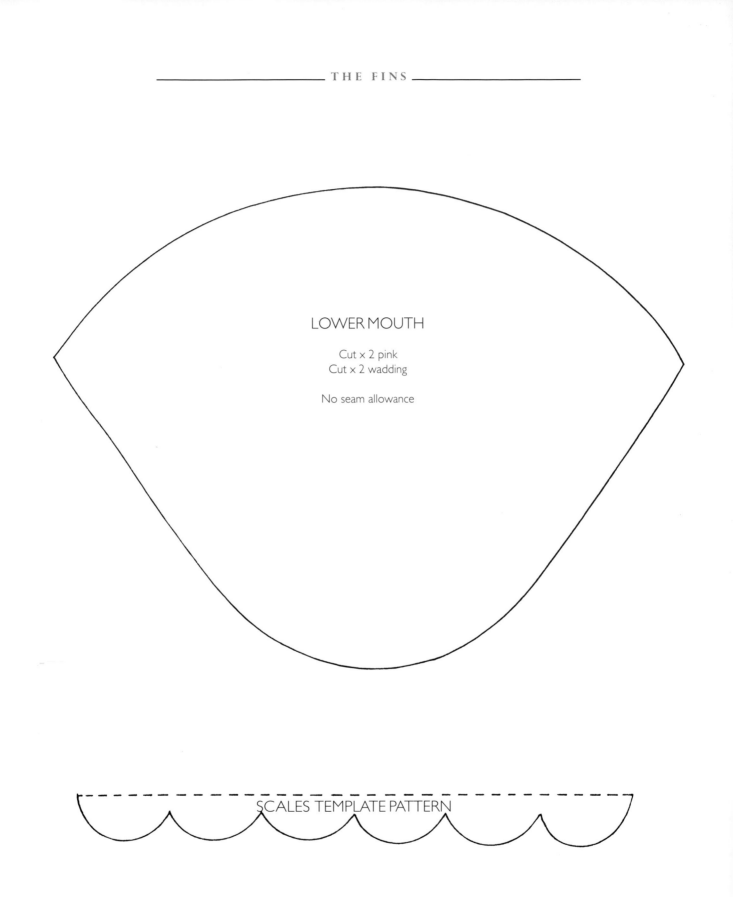

LOWER MOUTH

Cut x 2 pink
Cut x 2 wadding

No seam allowance

SCALES TEMPLATE PATTERN

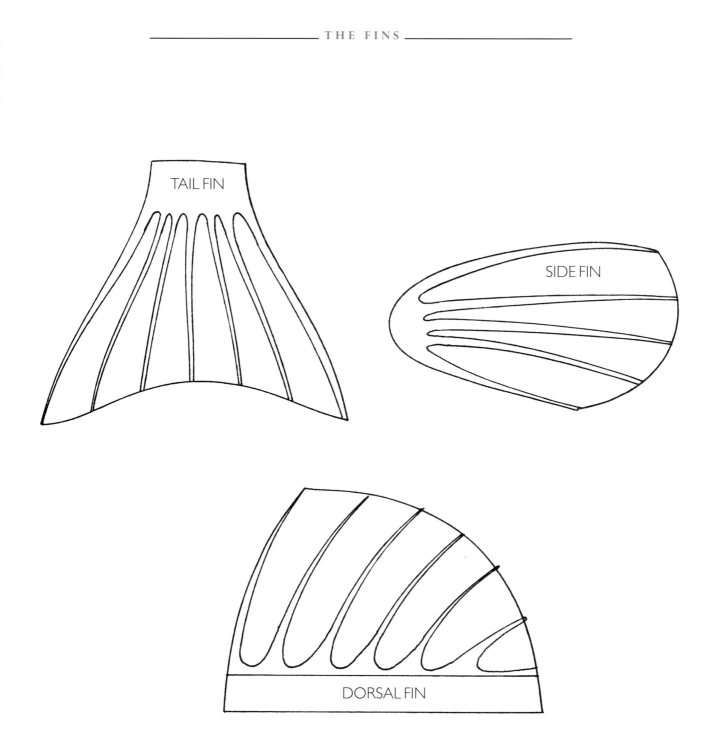

TAIL FIN

SIDE FIN

DORSAL FIN

Tutti
&
Frutti

Carmen Miranda's slippers were almost as famous as her hats. It's just that people always forgot to look down. So here they are, slices of life straight from Hollywood to provide a fruit cocktail cultivated for the cultivated.

You'll want to squeeze the last drop out of these little cuties.

INSTRUCTIONS

MATERIALS

pair of full slippers

30 cm (12 in) bright blue cotton or wool fabric

felt craft pieces (24 cm x 30 cm (9½ in x 12 in))

two each light orange and white

one each medium orange, dark orange, light green,

medium green and dark green

light green thread

iron on webbing paper

30 small (6 mm long [¼ in]) seed pearls

10 cm (4 in) of 5 mm (³⁄₁₆ in) thick fleece, firm wadding or thick felt

■ Following Method 2 or 3 on page 11 or 12, cover slippers.

■ Press light orange and light green felt squares onto web paper.

■ Trace large Orange Slice shape onto paper on orange felt 22 times and Lime Slice shape onto paper on pale green felt 26 times.

■ Cut out along outlines and then broken lines one at a time and press segments on to white felt, spreading segments out a little so there is space of about 2 mm (¹⁄₁₆ in) between them.

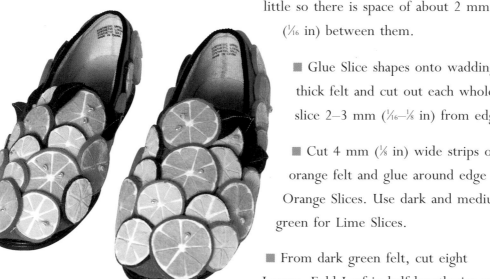

■ Glue Slice shapes onto wadding or thick felt and cut out each whole slice 2–3 mm (¹⁄₁₆–⅛ in) from edge.

■ Cut 4 mm (⅛ in) wide strips of orange felt and glue around edge of Orange Slices. Use dark and medium green for Lime Slices.

■ From dark green felt, cut eight Leaves. Fold Leaf in half lengthwise and stitch narrow dart (to suggest centre vein) to within 1 cm (⅜ in) of tip. Open out and from right side, using light green thread topstitch just next to seamline from leaf base to leaf point.

■ Arrange Slices on slippers starting at heel and overlapping towards the toe. Do not overlap on inside of instep or they may catch on opposite slipper when the wearer walks.

■ Slip Leaves under Slices around front of slipper opening.

■ Glue all pieces in place.

■ Glue seed pearls at points of segments randomly (about 15 per slipper).

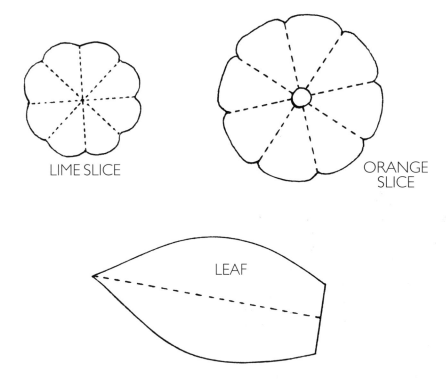

LIME SLICE

ORANGE SLICE

LEAF

Push
&
Pull

These vessels for the feet are extremely handi-
crafts, whether you agree with our Red and
Mercantile Aqua Marine colour choice or opt for
the Merchant Navy. Our toe-boats leave all
others in their wakes, housing you comfortably
in their forecastles as they ferry you from ship
to shore, shop to store. From dab hand with
needle and thread to deckhands on slippers that
are ship shape, these are craft of which to be
proud. Fore shore.

INSTRUCTIONS

MATERIALS

pair of full slippers

40 cm (½ yd) of red drill

sufficient black drill from which to cut 10 cm (4 in) wide strip

160 cm (1¾ yd) long or two 80 cm (31½ in) lengths

10 cm (4 in) of white drill

20 cm (8 in) beige corduroy

one each of black and blue felt craft pieces

24 cm x 30 cm (9½ in x 12 in)

60 cm (⅔ yd) white tape, 5 mm (¼ in) wide

50 cm (½ yd) fusible wadding

25 mm (1 in) thick foam for bridge

twelve 11 mm (⅜ in) gold eyelets

scrap of shiny black fabric for backing eyelets

6 m (6½ yd) narrow white cord

60 cm (⅔ yd) black cord

white pencil

polyester fibre filling

pair of anchors

RAILING

■ Using white pencil, draw a straight line along the centre of the strip of black drill. With white thread and a narrow zig zag stitch, sew a length of thin white cord along the line. Using the machine foot as a spacing guide, stitch 2 more lengths of white cord on each side of the first. Fold strip in half lengthwise with central cord along the fold. Using white thread and a straight stitch, sew in a crenellated pattern across the strip to form posts (uprights) at approximately 1.5 cm (⅝ in)

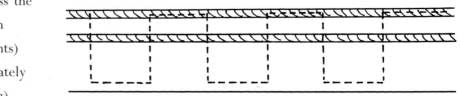

intervals, adjusting stitch length so that 6 stitches covers the distance exactly between posts.

SHIP SIDES

■ Check pattern for fit around sole of slippers. Use photocopier to enlarge or reduce pattern to fit, making same adjustment to all pattern pieces.

■ From red drill adding 1.5 cm (⅝ in) seam allowance to all edges, cut a pair each of Inside and Outside. On right side of fabric, mark positions for portholes (marked with Xes on the diagram) and white line. Place white tape in position at white line and topstitch along both sides of tape.

■ From corduroy adding 1.5 cm (⅝ in) seam allowance, cut pair of Deck and two pairs of Deck Bands.

■ From wadding, cut Sides, Deck and Deck Band pieces without seam allowance. Fuse wadding to wrong side of all pieces.

■ Insert eyelets for portholes where marked. From the back, glue scraps of shiny black fabric over the rim of each eyelet.

■ With right sides together, stitch centre front seam at bow.

■ Matching raw edges, stitch Railing to top edge of right side of Sides.

DECK

■ With machine stitching, reinforce corner A and C on Deck piece. With right sides together, stitch short ends of Deck Band to each side of Deck. With right sides together, stitch Deck to Sides stopping 3 cm (1¼ in) from centre back on each side. Join centre back seam on Sides including rail then on Deck Band. Hand stitch the remaining join of Deck to Sides. Glue a small piece of black felt in place to disguise the seam on the Rail.

BRIDGE

■ From foam, cut a pair of Bridges. From white drill, adding seam allowance, cut a pair of Bridge Tops and Bridge Sides. With right sides together, join ends of Bridge Side to form a ring. With right sides together, join Bridge Side to Bridge Top with seam of Bridge Side positioned at the mid point of one side, clipping into Bridge Side at corners to turn more easily. Trim seam and turn to right side. Insert foam piece then turn edges under and hand stitch in place. The seam of the Bridge Side is the centre back of the Bridge.

FUNNEL

■ From black felt, cut a pair of Funnel Tops and two 13 cm x 15 cm (5 in x 6 in) rectangles. From blue felt, cut two 6.5 cm x 15 cm (2½ in x 6 in) rectangles. Place blue felt over black felt, with top edge of blue, 8 cm (3¼ in) below top edge of black. Lower edge of blue will overlap black by 1.5 cm (⅝ in). Stitch along top edge of blue. Place white tape over this join and topstitch along both sides of tape. With right sides together, join side seam and turn to right side. This seam line is the centre back of the Funnel.

■ Hand stitch Funnel Top to top edge of black. Push Funnel top inside Funnel for about 3 cm (1¼ in). Turn lower blue edge to the wrong side 1.5 cm (⅝ in) and topstitch along the fold line, close to edge.

■ Fill with polyester fibre and hand stitch to centre of Bridge.

FINISHING OFF

■ Glue Bridge to Deck 1.5 cm (⅝ in) forward of deck/foot opening. Glue black cord over join between Bridge and Deck.

■ From black felt, cut out Windows and glue to sides of Bridge. The

Door goes on rear of the Bridge, to the left on the left foot and to the right on the right foot.

■ Make a coil of white cord and glue to Deck with a length hanging over the outer side of tug boat. Glue anchor to the end and fix to Side of boat.

■ Turn under lower edges of Sides 1.5 cm (⅝ in) and glue in place on slipper just above sole, pushing some filling into the space between toe of slipper and underside of Deck. Glue or sew all loose parts of Deck to outside of slipper.

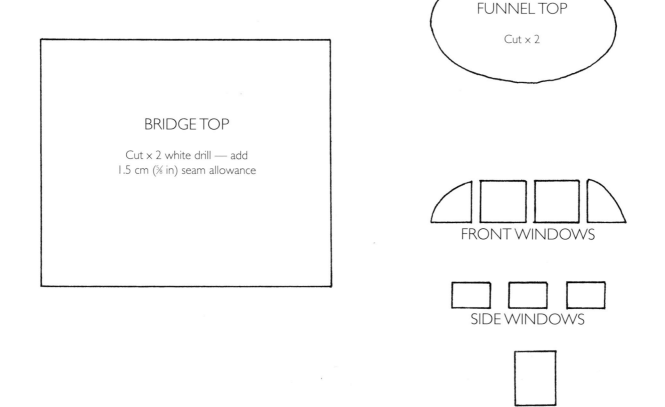

FUNNEL TOP

Cut × 2

BRIDGE TOP

Cut × 2 white drill — add
1.5 cm (⅝ in) seam allowance

FRONT WINDOWS

SIDE WINDOWS

DOOR

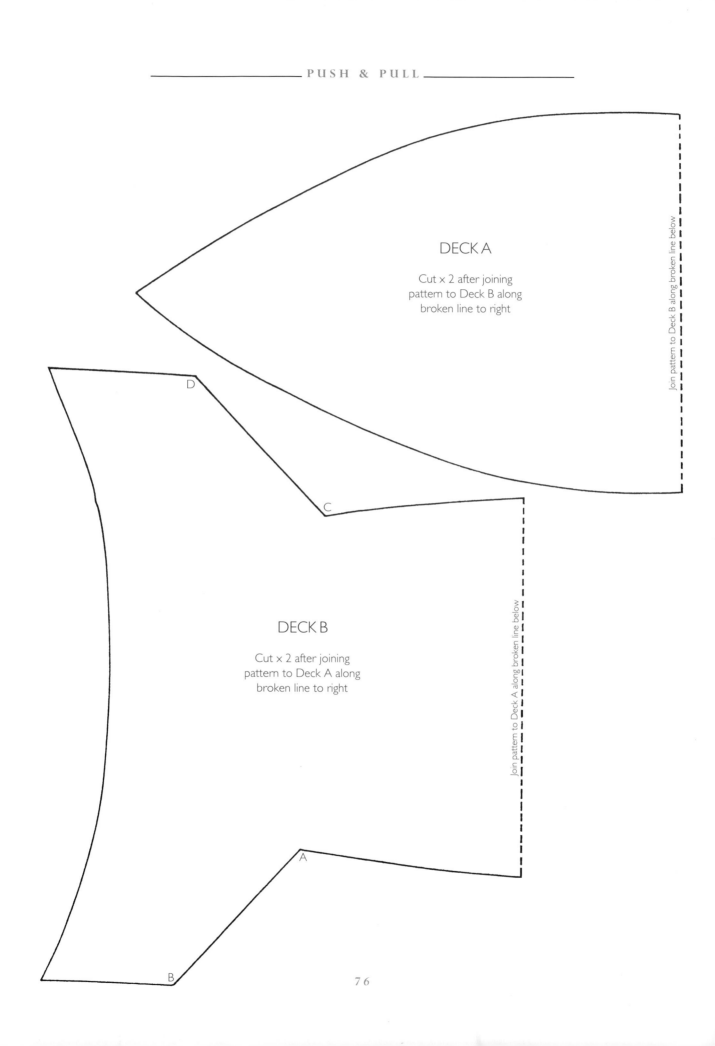

DECK A

Cut × 2 after joining
pattern to Deck B along
broken line to right

Join pattern to Deck B along broken line below

D

C

DECK B

Cut × 2 after joining
pattern to Deck A along
broken line to right

Join pattern to Deck A along broken line below

A

B

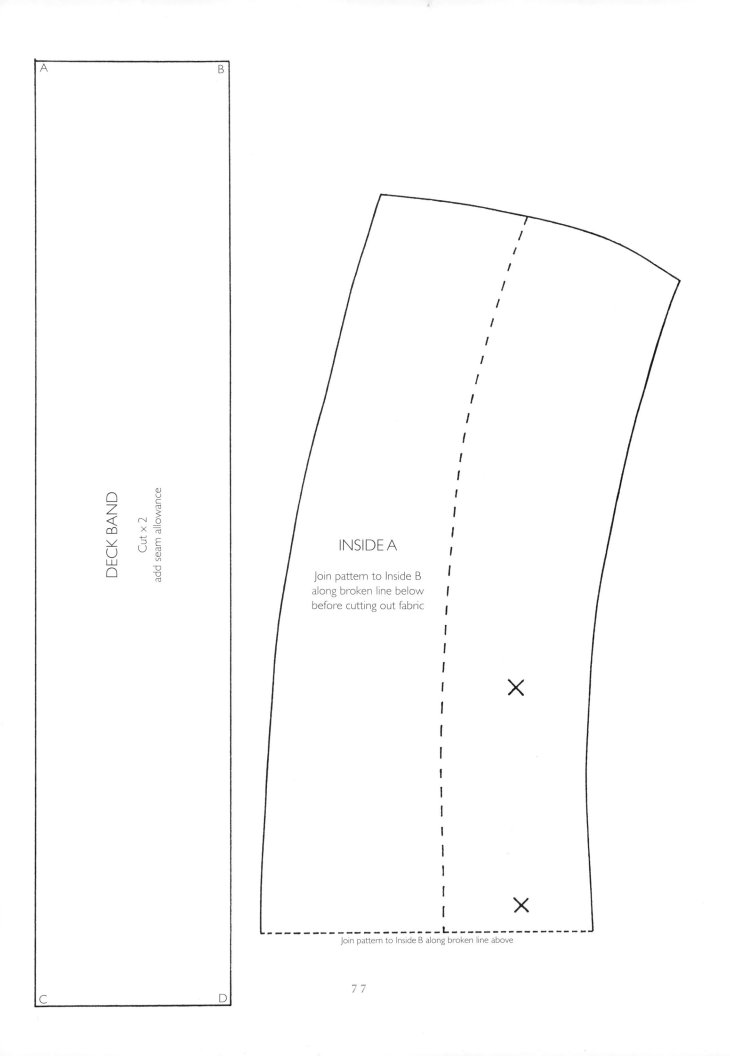

A   B

DECK BAND

Cut x 2

add seam allowance

C   D

INSIDE A

Join pattern to Inside B
along broken line below
before cutting out fabric

✕

✕

Join pattern to Inside B along broken line above

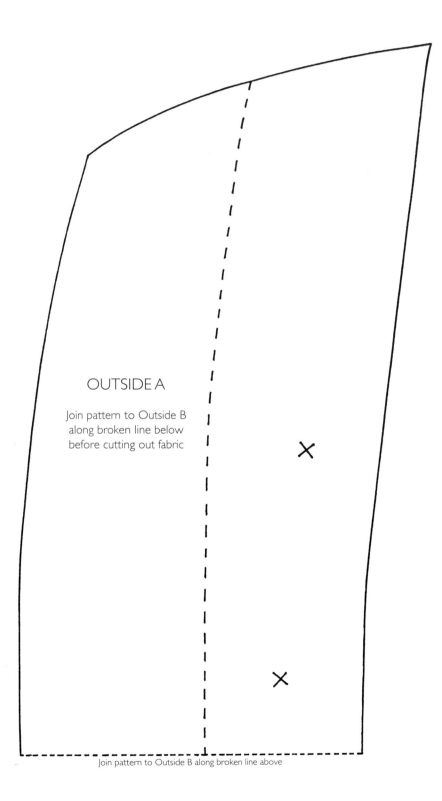

OUTSIDE A

Join pattern to Outside B
along broken line below
before cutting out fabric

Join pattern to Outside B along broken line above

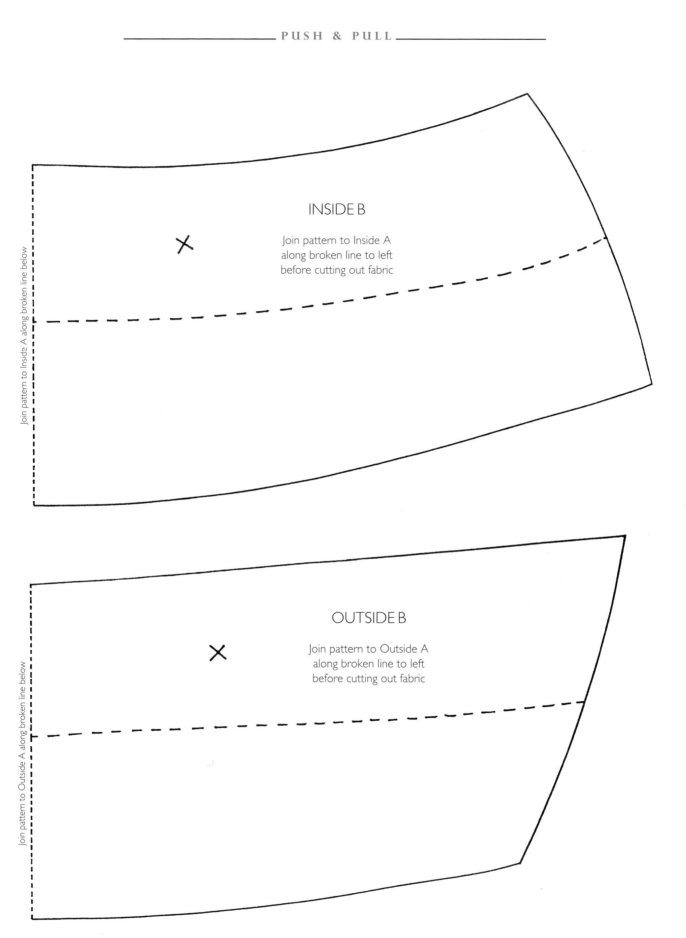

INSIDE B

Join pattern to Inside A
along broken line to left
before cutting out fabric

Join pattern to Inside A along broken line below

OUTSIDE B

Join pattern to Outside A
along broken line to left
before cutting out fabric

Join pattern to Outside A along broken line below

Seen on the Rialto

Shaped like gondolas, these are the crowned feet of Europe ready to power you under the bridge of thighs and straight to the palazzo.

From ermine-trimmed heels to toe-groping extremities, these slippers are the power beneath the throne. Nice attire in which to trip the light fantastic at a masked ball and comfy as well.

INSTRUCTIONS

MATERIALS

pair of full slippers

20 cm (8 in) gold satin fabric

20 cm (8 in) blue satin fabric

20 cm (8 in) red velvet

scrap purple felt

scrap black felt

scrap of interfacing

10 pearls

10 cm (4 in) fur fabric white with black dots

30 cm (12 in) wadding

small amount of polyester fibre filling

10 cm (4 in) black cotton fabric

purple thread

black thread

■ Following the principle of Method 2 on page 11 or 3 on page 12, make pattern for slipper cover in two pieces only with centre back seam, a seam down the centre front and no side seams. There will be an Inside and an Outside pattern piece. Do not curve the centre front seam over the toe.

■ Extend the centre front seam from the toe for about 5 cm (2 in) for an adult, 3 cm (1⅛ in) for a child. Draw a curve from the lower edge seam to meet the point. Make this toe extension to match on both Inside and Outside patterns.

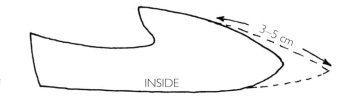

■ On the Inside, draw a line about half way between instep edge and toe of slipper from centre front seam to sole and cut along this line to give a Toe piece and an Inside Side piece. Add 1.5 cm seam allowance to all edges of the pattern pieces. From blue satin, cut one pair of Outside, from gold satin, cut one pair of Inside Side and from red velvet, cut one pair of Toe. Join all the seams except for the centre back.

■ With right sides together, place the point of the toe over the black cotton fabric for the distance the toe will extend past the end of the slipper and stitch together 1.5 cm from the edge. Trim off excess black fabric and turn to right side.

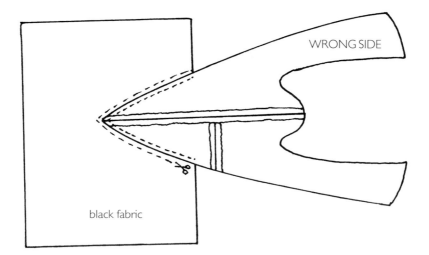

WRONG SIDE

black fabric

■ Glue a layer of thin wadding over the slippers, trimming close to the edge and fit the cover over this. Pin the back seam to fit, mark, remove cover and stitch back seam where marked.

■ Put some filling into the point of toe. Press bottom edges to inside and put the cover back onto the slipper. Glue bottom edge in place and glue the front wherever it sits comfortably. Trim excess from the top edge flush with the slipper and bind with a 5 cm (2 in) wide strip of fur with the nap of the fur running towards the sole.

CROWN

■ Make a pattern for Crown and Point. Place purple felt over interfacing and trace a pair of Crowns. Using purple thread, stitch just inside the line and cut out on traced line. Using black felt over interfacing, trace, stitch and cut four points. Glue the black Points under the Crown so all the points are the same height. Glue or sew the crown onto the slipper over the junction of the seams and stitch a pearl at the top of each point.

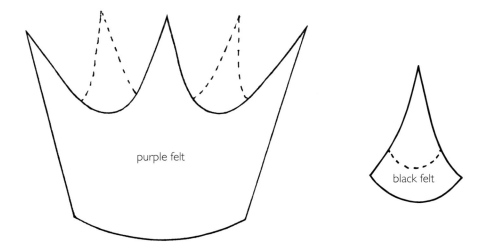

purple felt

black felt

Buzz
&
Swat

Tastefully modelled beside the garbage bin, this brilliant, if pestilential, pair are bound to rate a standing ovation at your next 'at home'.

Head, thorax and abdomen above the common *Musca domestica,* these glamorous creatures will amaze your friends and blow your enemies away.

INSTRUCTIONS

MATERIALS

pair of full slippers

50 cm (½ yd) of bright fabric to cover slippers if desired

2 x 4.3 cm (1¾ in) diameter tea infusers (for eyes)

10 cm x 20 cm (4 in x 8 in) scrap black Lycra

10 cm x 20 cm (4 in x 8 in) black velvet

10 cm x 20 cm (4 in x 8 in) black vinyl

10 cm x 60 cm (4 in x 24 in) white tulle

10 cm x 60 cm (4 in x 24 in) grey organza

10 cm x 60 cm (4 in x 24 in) fusing web

10 cm x 50 cm (4 in x 20 in) shining green fabric e.g. lamé

black and grey thread

6 fine pipe cleaners, 21 cm (8¼ in) long

hot glue gun and glue pellets

scrap stiff cardboard

20 cm x 60 cm (8 in x 24 in) fine wadding

about 1 cm (⅜ in) thick

handful of polyester fibre filling

■ If slippers require covering follow Method 3 on page 12.

■ Trace pattern and check that fly fits over toe of slipper; if not adjust size with a photocopier. From cardboard, cut out Head and Thorax without seam allowance. Adding 1.5 cm (⅝ in) seam allowance, cut one of Head from lycra and one of Thorax from velvet. Glue cardboard Head and Thorax pieces to a square of wadding then trim wadding to fit them. Cover the Head with lycra on top of the wadding and glue the edges of the fabric to the cardboard side. Repeat this process with the Thorax using the velvet, leaving the front edge open to accommodate the Head.

■ Glue narrow end of Head to Thorax.

WINGS

■ Place a layer of fusible web between organza and tulle and fuse, pressing on tulle side with a pressing cloth to protect iron.

■ Trace Wing including veins onto tulle side. Flop pattern and trace onto tulle side again to make a pair of wings. Using grey thread and a narrow machine satin stitch, sew vein lines. Cut out Wings and glue under the back of the Thorax as shown on the full illustration.

■ From vinyl cut out the Abdomen and glue in place to Thorax, leaving Wings free once they emerge from Thorax.

EYES

■ From green fabric cut four 10 cm (4 in) diameter circles, run a gathering thread around edge of each and pull up taking in a little filling to form a ball.

■ Dismantle tea infusers to give four strainers. Place a fly in position on the front of a slipper and slip a strainer with a green ball inside under each eye socket. Remove fly and hand stitch the strainers in place on slipper.

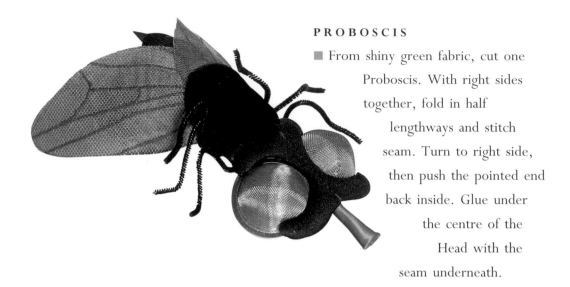

PROBOSCIS

■ From shiny green fabric, cut one
Proboscis. With right sides
together, fold in half
lengthways and stitch
seam. Turn to right side,
then push the pointed end
back inside. Glue under
the centre of the
Head with the
seam underneath.

LEGS

■ Arrange the pipe cleaners under the Thorax and glue or sew to the edge of Thorax at each side. Glue a small roll of wadding under Thorax and Abdomen to keep body rounded.

■ Glue or sew fly to slipper, so the Head encircles an eye on each side. Bend legs into shape and either leave ends free or catch them down with a stitch if desired.

■ Catch wings down with a few stitches.

ASSEMBLED
FLY

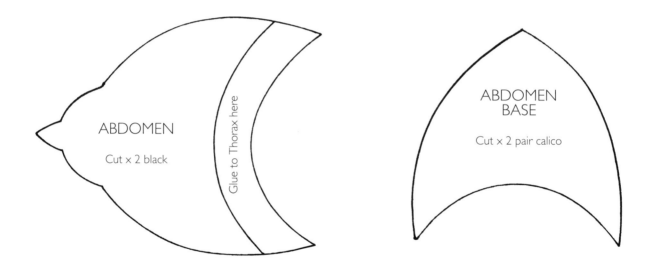

ABDOMEN

Cut x 2 black

Glue to Thorax here

ABDOMEN
BASE

Cut x 2 pair calico

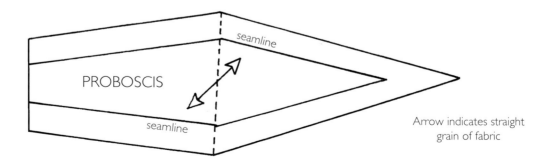

PROBOSCIS

seamline

seamline

Arrow indicates straight
grain of fabric

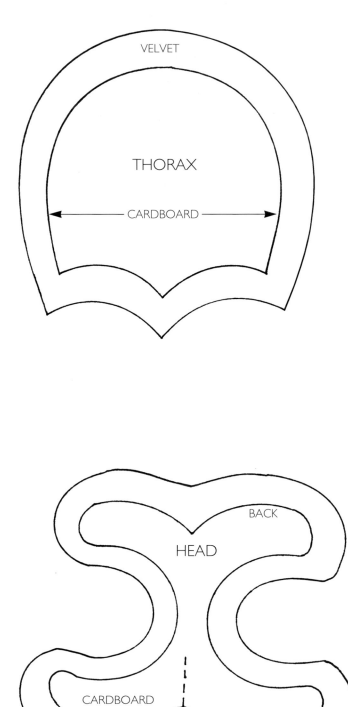

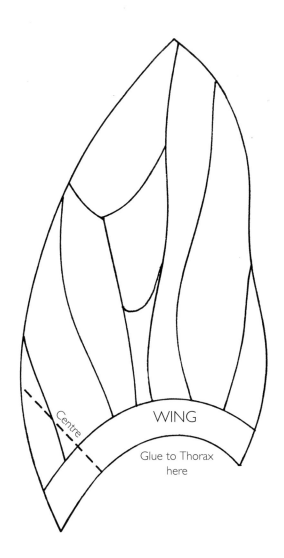

Way down upon the...

If you spend your time swanning through the shallows of life looking for a Leda, then these could be for you: a pair of slippers to take the waddle out of your walk and put glide in your stride.

You may also feel moved to constant primping and preening but beware of the swan uppers — they'll always put you down.

INSTRUCTIONS

MATERIALS

pair of full slippers in black or navy

(slipper is visible at the back, below the tail of the swan)

50 cm (½ yd) of white velvet

50 cm (½ yd) of white felt

50 cm (½ yd) white bias binding, 25 mm (1 in) wide

30 cm (12 in) wadding

scrap of red felt

scrap of black felt

two pairs of eyes, 7.5 mm (⁵⁄₁₆ in) in diameter

white feathers, about 60 around 7 cm (2¾ in) long

fusible web paper

■ Following general principles of Method 2 on page 11 or 3 on page 12, make pattern for slipper cover in two pieces only with centre back seam, a seam down the centre front and no side seams. There will be an Inside and an Outside pattern piece.

■ Add Head/Neck pattern to centre front edge of both patterns and remove Tail cut-out area, making sure the Inside and Outside patterns will fit properly together. Mark point D at centre front instep.

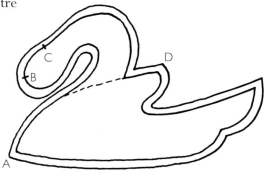

■ Add a 1 cm (⅜ in) seam allowance to all edges.

■ From velvet, cut out pair each of Inside, Outside and Head Gusset. Mark stitching line on wrong side. With right sides together, join seams between A-B and C-D. Sew in gusset matching B-B and C-C. Turn right side out.

■ From white felt, cut out pair each of Inside and Outside Body patterns omitting the Head and Neck. Join centre front seam leaving a 5 cm (2 in) opening 5 cm (2 in) from the sole line. Press seam open.

■ With right sides together, pin felt piece to velvet piece. Pin a piece of wadding to felt side of the back half of both sides, folding the Head out of the way.

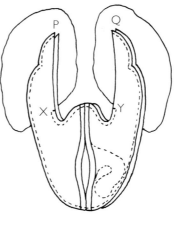

■ Stitch between X and Y, P and Q. Clip seam at X and Y trim, clip corners and curves, then turn to right side.

■ Open out binding, fold in half lengthwise and press. With binding on velvet side, match raw edges and stitch binding in place from X to P and Q to Y.

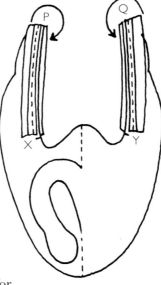

■ Use polyester fibre to fill head and neck then continue to fill front of swan between felt and velvet.

■ Place the swan over the slipper and pin it in place. Glue it down around the sole and tail.

■ Hand stitch the binding to the inside of the slipper.

■ From felt, cut out two pairs of Wings for each swan. From wadding, cut one pair. Join wings in pairs with a layer of wadding on one side. Stitch around the edge, leaving an opening between S and T then turn to the right side.

■ Place feathers on wing starting at the curved end, extending back about 5 cm (2 in) and glue to hold. Continue layering the feathers

until the Wing is covered. Glue the wings in position on the swan to cover the elastic on the slippers.

■ Iron some fusible web paper to the black felt and trace the Upper Black Beak and Lower Black Beak patterns on paper side. Repeat with the red felt and Red Beak patterns. Cut out all beak pieces. Peel paper off the red pieces only and press each red piece onto the corresponding black piece.

■ With red sides together stitch the Upper and Lower parts together. Turn to right side to form the beak. Attach eyes in position and glue or sew Beak to head.

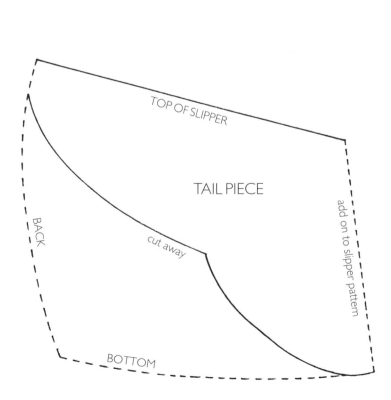

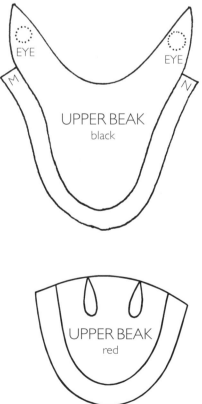

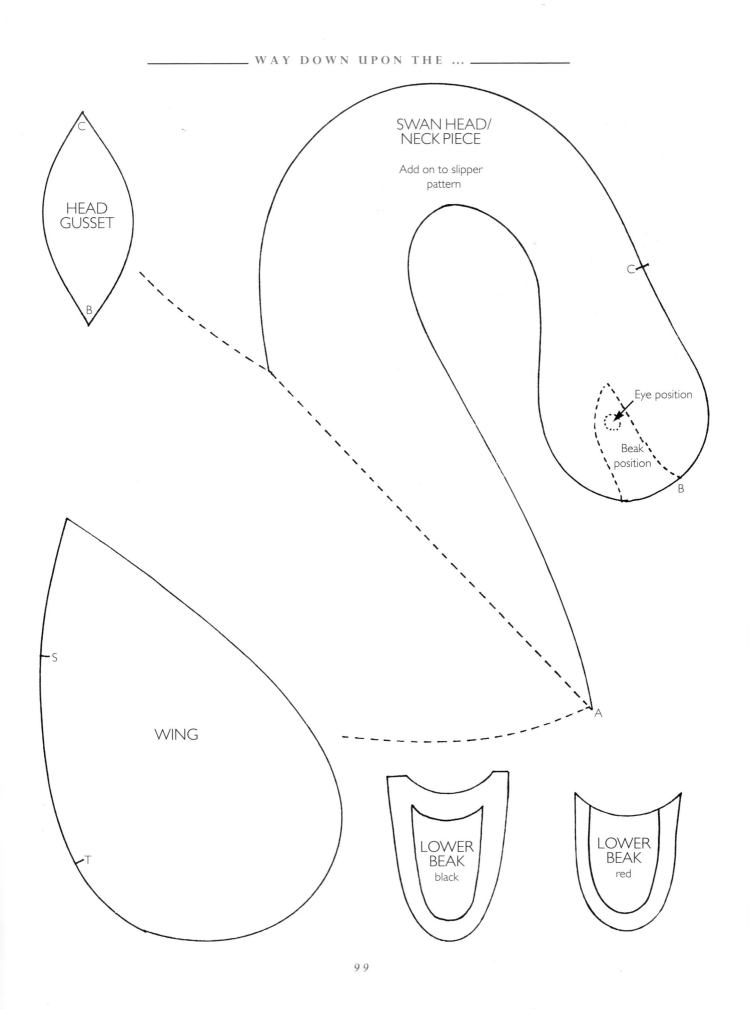

HEAD
GUSSET

SWAN HEAD/
NECK PIECE

Add on to slipper
pattern

Eye position

Beak
position

WING

LOWER
BEAK
black

LOWER
BEAK
red

The Missionary Decision

Inspired by Margaret Mead, you are proselytising in Polynesia, but worry about baring your sole.

Don't worry. No self-respecting cannibal ever ate a missionary's shoes.

These slippers could be your token totem — on your feet if not on the wall.

INSTRUCTIONS

MATERIALS

pair of full slippers with elastic inserts

60 cm (⅔ yd) black fabric or felt for covering slippers

scrap black felt if not used for slippers

20 cm (8 in) white felt

20 cm (8 in) gold felt

thread, one each of black, gold and white black

4 cowrie shells

2 m (2¼ yd) string

paper backed fusible web

natural coloured raffia

PREPARING SLIPPERS

■ Cover the back of the slippers. Following Method 2 on page 11, make pattern to cover back of slippers, extending the inside and outside back panels about 5 cm into the front section of the slippers. Cut pieces from black fabric and cover the back of the slippers.

■ Adjust Front cover pattern to fit comfortably on front of slipper. From black fabric, cut out Front and Facing.

MAKING MASK

■ Trace Mask pattern onto paper side of web paper and cut roughly around edge.

■ Press onto gold felt, paper side up, and cut out mask carefully. Remove paper and press mask onto white felt.

■ Press web paper onto the other side of white and trim it all back to about 3 mm (⅛ in) from the edge of the gold felt.

■ Trace Eye Surrounds onto web paper, press web paper onto white felt, cut out and press in position on gold felt Mask, then topstitch.

■ Remove paper from back of Mask and press onto Front slipper cover.

■ Sew dart and press open.

■ With right sides together, and matching notches, stitch Facing to Front. Clip seam, turn to right side.

■ Topstitch the instep edge.

MAKING EYES

■ The black parts of the eyes are raised and, as a result, they have sides like miniature circular box-sided cushions.

■ Cut out Eye and Eye Side pieces from black felt. Build up Eye piece to 5 mm (¼ in) from behind with several layers of scrap felt.

■ Glue Eye Side strips around edge.

■ Glue or sew cowrie shells into centre of eyes. Glue or sew eyes to mask so that shells slant a little as in photograph.

FRONT

■ Place Front on slipper so that it covers slipper front entirely including elastic if necessary. Trim edge to 1.5 cm (⅝ in).

■ Turn edge under and glue or sew.

■ Push a little wadding or stuffing into bridge of nose area to give the mask more definition and glue or sew facing to top of slipper to secure.

FINISHING OFF

■ Make about 1 m (3 ft 4 in) of fringing by cutting raffia into 15 cm (6 in) lengths and knotting these to a string stretched between two chairs. Press fringe flat and trim to 5 cm (2 in).

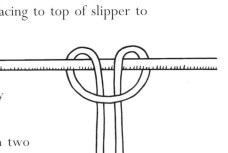

RAFFIA KNOT

■ Glue or sew fringe around back edge of slipper, turning loose ends of string under. Cut a 10 cm (4 in) length and glue fringe a little below chin of mask.

■ With scissors, round off ends of this piece of fringe as in the photograph.

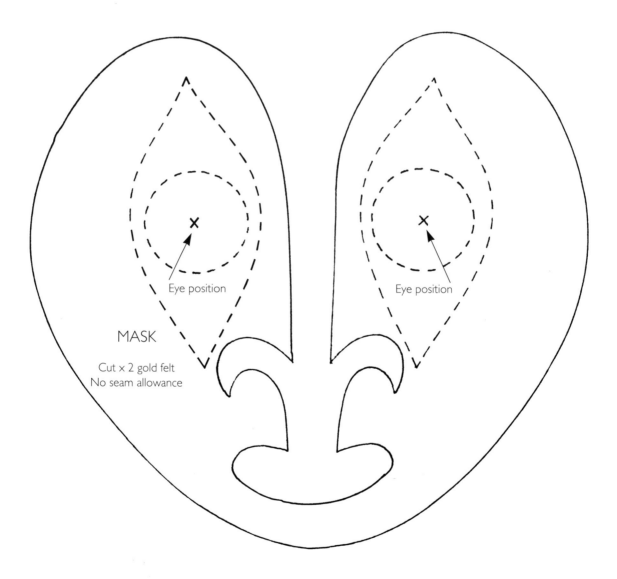

Eye position

Eye position

MASK

Cut x 2 gold felt
No seam allowance

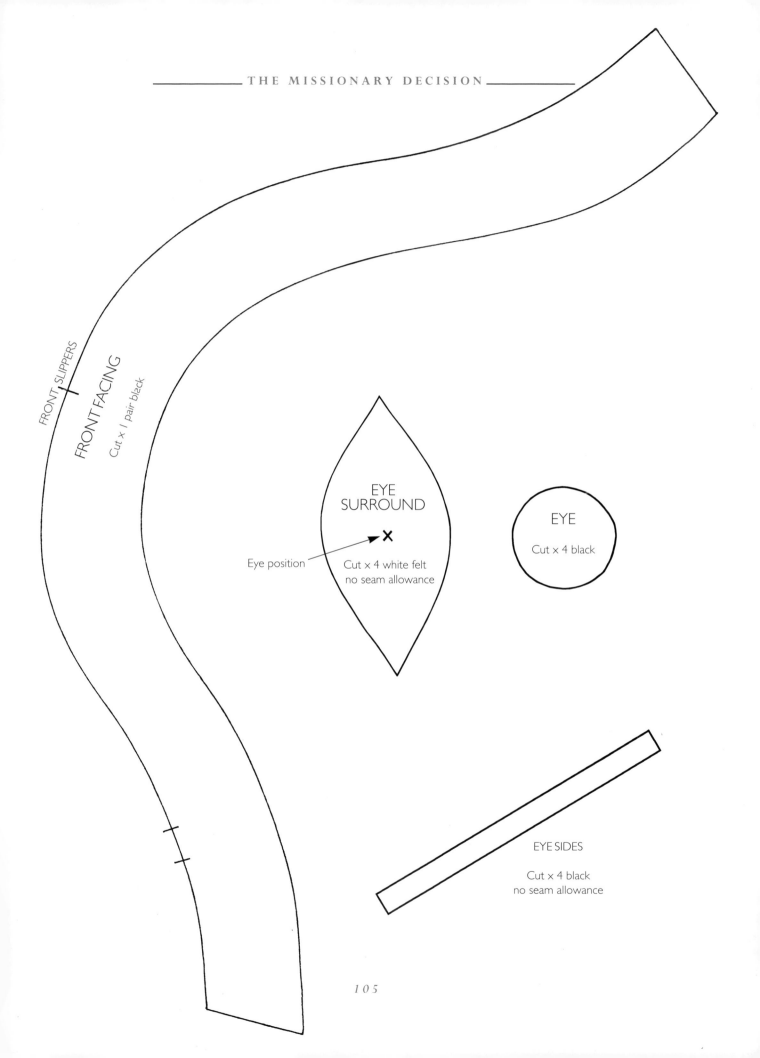

FRONT SLIPPERS

FRONT FACING

Cut x 1 pair black

EYE
SURROUND

Eye position ✗

Cut x 4 white felt
no seam allowance

EYE

Cut x 4 black

EYE SIDES

Cut x 4 black
no seam allowance

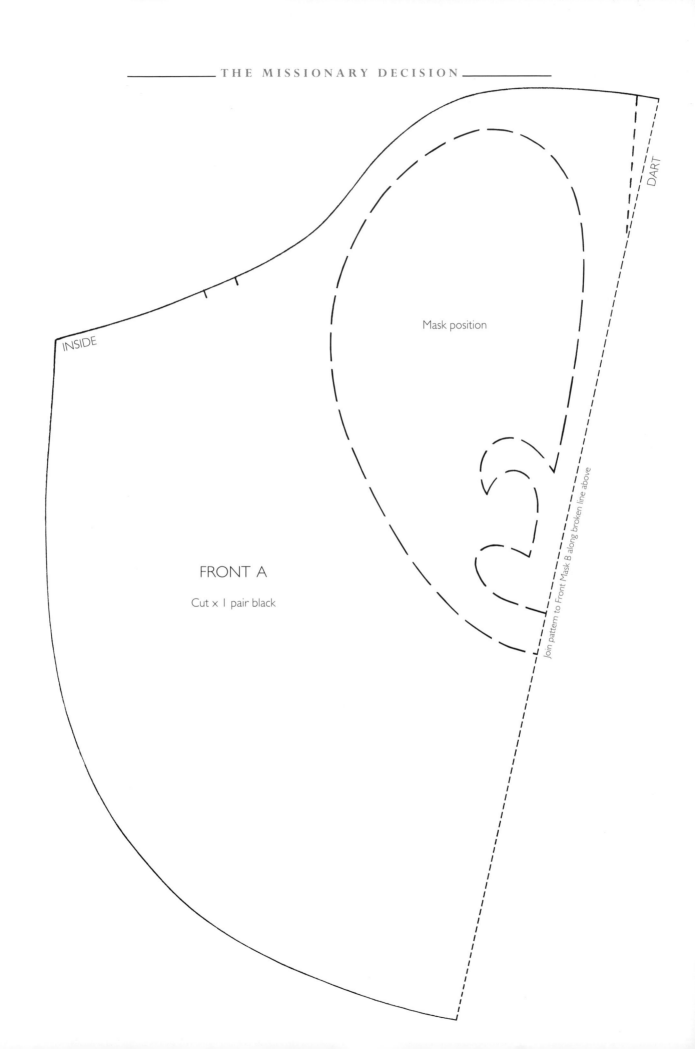

DART

Mask position

INSIDE

FRONT A

Cut × 1 pair black

Join pattern to Front Mask B along broken line above

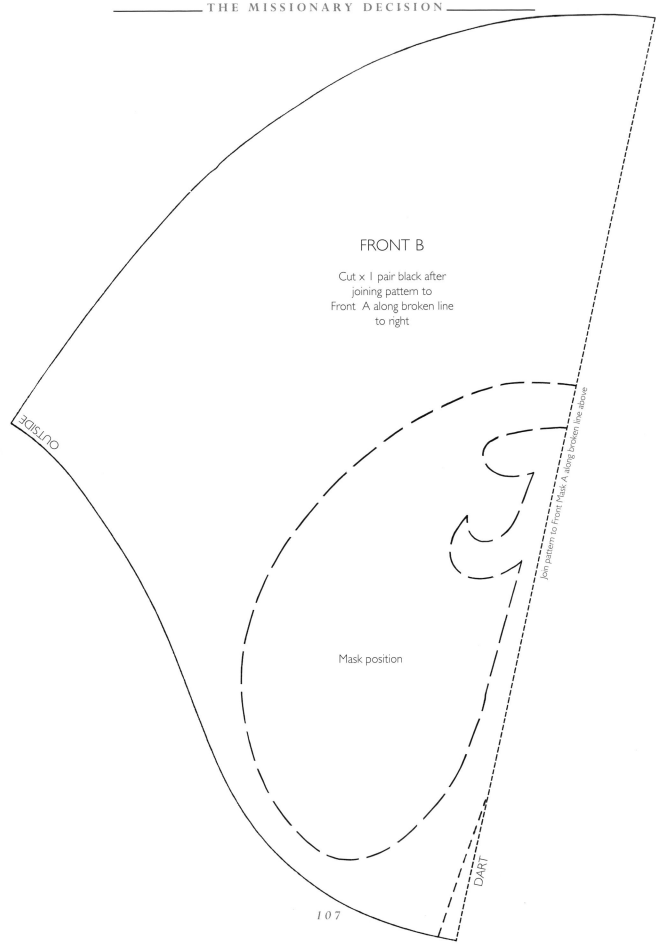

FRONT B

Cut x 1 pair black after
joining pattern to
Front A along broken line
to right

OUTSIDE

Join pattern to Front Mask A along broken line above

Mask position

DART

Initial
Pleasures

Drop your tools on the production line and take up needle and thread to create these very personal effects. These buttoned-down cross-stitched linen labels will win great approval from school matrons and nanny types. As well, they bear the footprint of the rugged individual; the outsider who is always be-slippered inside. Make them monograms or make a statement in just two letters; philosophise but be extremely brief; wax succinctly lyrical. This pair is for those who don't need a rank and serial number to know who they are.

INSTRUCTIONS

MATERIALS

pair of dark coloured slippers and fabric to cover if desired

10 cm x 20 cm (4 in x 8 in) white 36 count even weave linen

white thread

red stranded embroidery thread

tapestry needle (blunt point) size 24

8 pearl buttons, 10 mm (⅜ in) diameter

PREPARING SLIPPERS

■ Cover pair of slippers if desired.

MAKING LINEN PIECE

■ From linen, cut out two 7.5 cm (3 in) squares for medium slippers, adjusting the size for smaller or larger pairs. Hem all around, folding each edge over 3 mm (⅛ in) twice and slipstitching in place.

■ Find centre of square by folding in half twice to make a square and pinch folded corner with fingers. Open out. The pinched corner is the centre.

■ Using 2 strands of red thread and working in cross stitch over two threads, embroider initials centred over the pinched corner. Work each cross stitch individually and ensure that all the second (crossing) diagonal stitches of the letters go in the same direction.

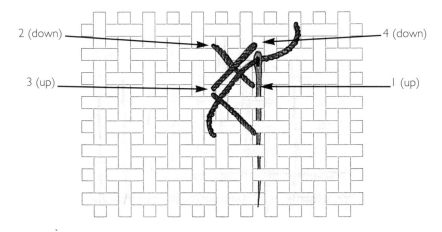

■ Make buttonholes running horizontally just inside the hem. Buttons should sit about 4 mm (³⁄₁₆ in) from the edges.

■ Arrange linen square on slipper and mark the position of buttons.

■ Sew buttons to slipper and button linen square in place.

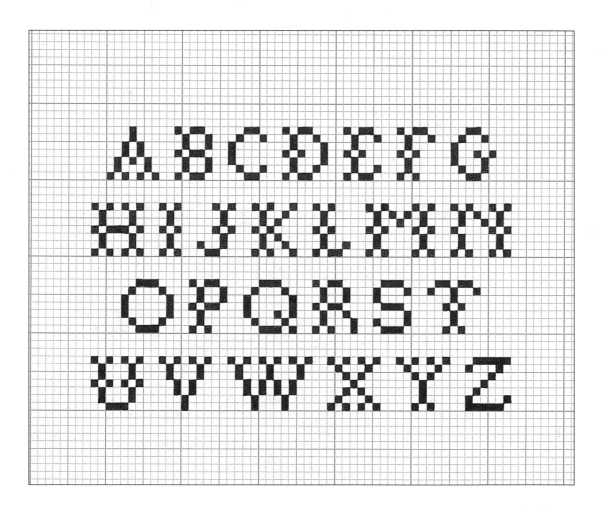